GUILTY
EXPLANATION

A Mostly True, Funny and Sad, Memoir About Growing Up and Growing Old

MARK W. SKALL

outskirts
press

TABLE OF CONTENTS

Chapter 1

GUILTY WITH AN EXPLANATION

My dad was Bernie Sanders; okay, not literally Bernie Sanders. However, he was Jewish like Bernie, and a socialist like Bernie. And by the way, his name was Bernie (Skall, not Sanders). Had Bernie Sanders been elected president, my father would have come back from the grave to watch his inauguration, doing back flips all the way.

Bernie Sanders is a nonpracticing Jew, but my father took it one step further: he didn't believe in God. Yup, my dad was a Jewish atheist. Despite not believing in God, my dad took tremendous pride in his Judaism, making jokes ("Are you ticklish or are you Jewish?") and chastising his children when we weren't being Jewish enough. For him Judaism was not a religion, but a culture, a club to which he and his family belonged. The other club was the *goyim*, a club he would rather die than join and who didn't want him for a member anyway.

I've always found it extremely curious that Jews break down the world population into two groups: Jews and non-Jews (*goys*). You're either a Jew or a *goy*, even though Jews make up only 1/5 of 1 percent of the world population. That's like saying there are two kinds of cars: 1962 Mercury Comets and all the other cars. By the way, did I mention that my dad's car was a 1962 Mercury Comet?

Besides Judaism, my dad's other passion was writing and

telling jokes. One of his favorite jokes became more prominent as he got older and, unfortunately, sicker. Whenever he saw a doctor for his Parkinson's disease, heart issues, or lung cancer, the nurses usually set him up in a room and asked him if he was comfortable. "I make a good living," he would always reply. In perfect health, or close to death from lung cancer, that joke was my dad's go-to line. He was an accountant by trade, but he always wanted to be a gag writer. He sent his jokes to Milton Berle or Jack Benny, waiting for the acceptance letter that never came. Instead, he received a form letter telling him that his jokes were good, but that Milton or Jack could not use them right now. Of course my dad would later swear that he heard one of the comedians telling his jokes and he always vowed to sue them for stealing his material.

For me, however, the funniest story associated with my dad was not a joke he told but a situation he got himself involved in. Ever since the 1950s, New York City has deployed a system known as alternate-side-of the-street parking. In this system, parked cars are restricted to one side of the street during certain hours on certain days. Signs are posted with the scheduled times and if drivers are not parked on the correct side of the street during these hours, they risk being ticketed or towed away. Parking tickets are quite common because drivers often forgot they have to move their car to the other side of the street. In arguably the dirtiest city in the world, the stated goal of alternate-side-of-the-street parking is to allow for the efficient cleaning of New York City streets, thus resulting in a cleaner city.

But alternate-side-of-the-street parking has not achieved its goal. Seventy or so years after its inception, one can stroll down any street and encounter mountains of trash bags and tons of litter emitting a disgusting smell that's unique to New York. If alternate-side-of the-street parking has not reduced the dirt and stench in the Big Apple, then why does it continue to exist?

Perhaps its real purpose is not to make the city cleaner, but to produce revenue through the inordinate number of parking tickets that are issued.

One of those parking tickets went to my dad. My family and I lived in the Linden Projects, a working-class housing project in the East New York section of Brooklyn. Although residents were not rich, to say the least, almost every family owned a car. Thus, like most areas in New York City, parking was at a premium. Once you found a parking space, you didn't want to give it up. Finding a spot close to your residence was an event to be celebrated. Although the objective of owning a car should be to use it to drive from place A to place B, knowing that your car was parked in a "good" spot tended to shift the objective of many New Yorkers from *driving* the car to *watching* the car stay in parking heaven as long as humanly possible. However, alternate-side-of-the-street parking made car *watching* exceedingly difficult. Nothing felt worse than having to get up from the couch every other day or so to give up a perfect parking space and look for one just as good on the opposite side of the street. So often my dad just wouldn't. He was too comfortable where he was. At other times, he meant to obey the law and move the car but just forgot or overslept. Many of those times, my dad was incredibly lucky because he went without receiving a parking citation for quite a while.

Then the inevitable happened. After basking in his incredibly great parking space, my dad, accompanied by my mom, my brother Robert, and me, went out to the car one beautiful spring day to go for a ride. We were going to spend the afternoon at a scenic state park eating sandwiches and throwing around a baseball. When we got close to the car, we saw the dreaded parking ticket. My dad had either intentionally or unintentionally forgotten to move the car to the other side of the street.

One of my dad's least desirable traits involved his propensity to try to push people to the limit in order to maximize his return. During a typical transaction he would never accept the first offer; he always bargained to get the best deal. But my dad didn't consider this trait undesirable. He was extremely proud of it. In fact, he viewed it as a way of obtaining justice for the downtrodden, since he always saw himself as the little man fighting the system. If he received unfavorable news regarding a monetary matter, he almost always tried to figure a way out of it.

In line with this philosophy, my dad immediately decided to figure out how to eliminate or reduce the amount of money he owed for parking illegally. In our building in the Linden Projects, we lived in apartment 6H. Our neighbors Shirley and Willy lived in apartment 6B, right down the hall from us. They were nice people with two young children, one for whom I babysat to earn a little extra money. While making small talk with Willy while babysitting, I learned that Willy was a clerk for a judge in the local traffic court in Brooklyn. I immediately realized that Willy could help in my dad's quest for "justice," so I told my dad about Willy's relationship with the court system.

The next evening, my dad went to speak to Willy. "Willy, I got screwed," said my dad. "The bastards are always trying to take money away from hard-working men like us."

"What happened?" asked Willy.

"They gave me a ticket because I didn't move my car during alternate-side-of-street parking hours. That's just bullshit. They don't clean the streets even when we move our cars, and even if they did, they're obviously not very good at it, because the streets are still filthy. This city is a pigsty."

"Yeah. All they ever want to do is screw us."

"Can I beat this ticket?" asked my dad.

"No way," said Willie. "But you can reduce the amount of money you'll pay."

"How do I do that?" asked my dad.

"It's easy. You just plead guilty with an explanation. They'll automatically reduce your fine. You'll pay half of the fine, at most."

"But what explanation should I use?"

"It doesn't matter. You can say anything. Judges never listen to what the explanation is."

"Anything?"

"Yes. Absolutely anything. I've heard thousands of crazy explanations."

A week later my dad went to court.

"How do you plead?" asked Judge Friedman.

"Guilty with an explanation," said my dad.

"What's your explanation?" asked the judge.

"The day I got the ticket was the little-known Jewish holiday of Tish'a B'av. I'm deeply religious, and I was praying all day. On that day Jews aren't allowed to drive, so I couldn't move my car to the other side of the street."

Judge Friedman glared at my dad and said, "I've been going to shul (synagogue) almost my entire life, and I know that *nobody* observes Tish'a B'av. In forty years on the bench, I've never heard a more stupid explanation. Pay double the fine!"

Chapter 2

ROB-BIT HAS A BEAUT-I-FUL VOICE

*a*ll parents have a favorite child. Of course they say they don't, but they do. "We love all of our children equally," they always say. However, deep down inside they prefer one over all the others just a teeny-weeny bit more. In our family the favorite was my brother, Robert.

I was a pretty smart kid and did very well in school. I got just about all A's. In New York City schools at that time, grades were numerical. The passing grade was 65, grades in the 70s were fair, grades in the 80s were good, and grades in the 90s were exceptional. My grades were always in the 90s. My brother's grades were in the 70s and 80s. I passed the test to get into one of the most prestigious high schools in the country, Stuyvesant High, and did very well there. My brother went to the neighborhood high school in Brooklyn (Jefferson High) and scraped through. I easily got into Brooklyn College, the most difficult free city college to get into, while my brother went to Baruch College, the easiest city college.

However, none of these things mattered to my mother.

"Mark gets good grades in school," my mother told everybody. "But Rob-bit has common sense." My mom's extreme New York accent was a joy to listen to. It caused her to pronounce my brother's name as two distinct syllables: *Rob* and *bit*.

For those of you who have ever argued with somebody and were presenting elegantly logical arguments only to be told by the other side that they have no logical arguments for their position but that their position "is just common sense," you know that one person's common sense is another person's rubbish.

Perhaps one of the reasons that my brother was the favorite was that he kissed up to everyone in the family. Whenever we had a gathering of aunts and uncles, Aunt Esther or Aunt Gertie or Aunt Ann would invariably ask my brother and me to come give them a kiss. After we kissed them, they always kissed us, happily, in return. When the return kisses were about to happen, I ran in the other direction. My brother, on the other hand, was only too happy to receive these big kisses and walk away with what looked like a tattoo of a woman's lips on his cheeks.

Robert was the sociable one and was always willing to appease and please my parents as well as our aunts and uncles. One way he pleased them was by singing.

"Rob-bit has a beaut-i-ful voice," my mother would say. "Rob-bit, sing something for everyone."

My brother would then break out in a chorus of "Easter Parade." I can still hear Robert joyously belting out the first line "In your Easter bonnet, with all the frills upon it."

Now, my uncle Max, my mom's brother, was a cantor and a rabbi and really did have a beautiful voice. For those of you who aren't familiar with the term, a cantor sings while leading people in prayer in weekly Shabbat and holiday Jewish religious services. Besides leading worship, cantors officiate at lifecycle events and often lead synagogue choirs. Many years later, Uncle Max performed my wedding ceremony.

Uncle Max took my brother under his wing and worked with him on his singing. My brother joined the choir in Uncle Max's synagogue and traveled to different venues, belting out Jewish songs, but to this day it mystifies me why my brother, who did all of his singing in Uncle Max's synagogue choir, would choose "Easter Parade" to sing to all the relatives.

Oftentimes siblings argue over which one is the favorite. Some brothers or sisters insist that they were the favorite. At other times, the insistence is that the other sibling was the favorite. As I said before, I was and still am absolutely convinced that my brother, Robert, was the favorite. Although my brother denies it, I'm quite sure he knows that it's true.

If I needed any more evidence of the favoritism toward my brother, it arrived one day out of the blue. About thirty years ago or so, I received a request from my parents. They were living in Florida at the time, and I was living in Maryland. They were planning a trip to Maryland to visit my wife, Diana, and me and wanted to show me a video they had taken long ago but had just recently found while cleaning their condo. It was a video of my brother and me.

When my brother and I were young, my parents had apparently owned an eight-millimeter motion-picture camera, and the old film they just found had been taken with this camera. However, they no longer owned a projector and wanted to know if I knew of anyone that had an eight-millimeter projector they could use to show me the film. I mentioned this request to our good friends Billy and Janet, and to my surprise, they said they had an eight-millimeter projector. The day after my parents arrived at our house in Maryland, I invited Billy and Janet to our house and asked them to bring the eight-millimeter projector with them.

Billy and I lived in neighboring buildings in the Linden Projects and have known each other since the age of thirteen. I've known Janet since we were both in our early twenties. Billy and Janet knew my parents and also knew my brother. They had both heard me complain about my parents' favoritism and had seen it, on occasion, firsthand. Thus, when I told them they were about to see films of my brother and me, I could see the anticipation on their faces.

Billy and Janet arrived at our house, and we immediately loaded the film onto the projector. We all gathered around the kitchen table, eagerly awaiting the show. In the first scene my brother, at a pretty young age, was on a swing in a beautiful park. The film traced my brother oscillating back and forth across that familiar arc while smiling broadly and waving. He seemed to be having a wonderful time and was enjoying the attention of being filmed.

"That's wonderful," said Janet. "But where's Mark?"

"He's there," said my mother.

"But where?" asked Janet.

"Can't you see?"

"No."

"Look at the hands pushing the swing. You can even see Mark's elbow."

My mother was not kidding. In her mind it was okay and certainly didn't demonstrate any favoritism to show my brother smiling, sitting on a swing, and clearly being the center of attention, with me as the supporting player, pushing the swing, with only my hands and part of my arm visible.

But the next scene was truly astounding. It took place at the beach. The camera showed men and women of all ages sitting on beach chairs and lying on blankets while children played in the sand, some of them building sandcastles. The camera then panned to the ocean where many people were wading into the choppy water, while others were diving into the waves or swimming peacefully. The camera eventually stopped panning and focused on my brother frolicking happily in the peaceful ripples made by the waves. My mother was right beside him, floating on her back, and beaming.

Again Janet asked, "Where's Mark?"

"Hold you horses," said my mom. "You'll see him soon."

Eventually the camera panned to the left, showing my father with a chagrined look on his face. He seemed to be pushing down on an object and making it go under water. After a closer inspection of the object, we realized that object was me!

I couldn't believe it. "What's going on?" I asked.

"Don't you remember the game you and Daddy played, where he'd push you underwater and you'd see how long you could hold your breath?"

"No."

"You used to love that game," said my mother.

"Did Daddy and Robert play that game?"

"No, Robert doesn't like being pushed underwater. It's too dangerous."

Obviously, Robert has common sense!

Chapter 3

MANTLE AND MARIS

My friends and I grew up in the 1960s. Sure, most of us were born in the mid 1940s, so we lived through the 1940s and 1950s, but the decade that we all remember vividly was the 1960s. The part of the '60s that I remember most vividly was my junior high school years

Even though I attended one of the most dangerous junior high schools in the city, my junior high school years were the best years of my life. I had two sets of friends: kids who lived in my building and the neighboring building in the Linden Projects and friends from my junior high school. The Linden Projects were so big that all my non-school friends lived in my building, 580 Stanley Avenue, or the building across the courtyard from us, 570 Stanley Avenue. In a city project that comprised nineteen buildings, some of which were eight-story buildings and some of which were fourteen-story buildings spread over thirty acres of land, literally all of my non-school friends came from just two eight-story buildings sitting right next to each other.

I had about six very close friends from those two buildings and at least another six casual friends whom we would "call on" if we needed more kids for playing ball. When we didn't have school, we got up around 10 a.m., ate and (sometimes) showered. Then we would "call on" our friends from my building or the one across from us. I really have no idea why we used the term "calling on" someone when we went to their apartment, rang the doorbell, and asked them to come out and play, but that's what we said. And play we did. Stickball, punchball, roofball, hit the penny, and box ball were just a few of the games we played. Add to these the more traditional games of basketball, baseball, softball, handball, and football, and you can see that we had a pretty full agenda. We played ball from the time we got up until it was dark; no stopping for eating, drinking, or bathroom breaks. On school days the ritual would be the same, except that the ball playing started when school let out, rather than in the late morning. Stickball was the game we played the most.

On October 1, 1961, major league baseball season's final day, Roger Maris hit his 61st home run of the year, breaking Babe Ruth's record for home runs in a season. During the season Roger Maris and Mickey Mantle both challenged Ruth's record but Mantle fell short with *only* 54 home runs.

While the whole country was fascinated watching Mantle and Maris chase Babe Ruth's record, my friends and I were in a record-breaking chase of our own. In that same year, 1961, Billy Epstein hit his 61st home run on August 29. But Billy's 61st home run was in stickball. Roger Maris hit his record-breaking 61st home run off of Tracy Stallard of the Boston Red Sox. Billy hit his 61st home run off of Freddy Cohen from the Linden Projects. By the time our stickball season ended in October 1961, I ended up with 81 home runs in stickball, but Billy edged me out for the home-run championship with 82. Although we were all aware of the battle between Mantle and Maris, the boys of the Linden Projects were much more concerned with the home-run battle in stickball between Billy Epstein and me.

Billy and I were best friends. Freddy Cohen was our third best friend in this unlikely triumvirate. Freddy was the nicest of us three. He would give the shirt off of his back to help us and just about everyone else. But he wasn't the best athlete around. Although he followed the stickball championship like the rest of us at 570/580 Stanley Avenue, Freddy didn't hit many home runs. Instead of keeping track of his home runs, Freddy kept track of his batting average, to four decimal places!

"I hit .3869 this year," Freddy would tell us. "Pretty good, huh?"

And .3869 would have been a very good batting average, *if you played in the major leagues* batting against a Whitey Ford curveball that looked like it was dropping off a table or a 100 mile-an-hour Bob Feller fastball. However, our stickball curveballs were limited by the softness of the rubber ball we played with, and our pathetic fastballs probably never topped out at more than 50 miles an hour. Billy and I never had the heart to tell Freddy that we both hit over .700 that year.

Stickball was and still is a game played in the streets, usually in large cities in the northeastern part of the country. New York and Philadelphia were the two cities where stickball was most popular. Stickball came to national prominence in 1951, when Willie Mays, then a rookie with the New York Giants, famously played stickball with kids in the streets of New York. Mays said that he learned to hit the curveball by playing stickball on 155th Street in Harlem, in the streets in between the cars.

In New York, stickball was typically played in one of two places—either in the streets (which we called gutters) or in a schoolyard. The only participants needed in a game of stickball were the hitter, the pitcher, at most one fielder, and (sometimes) a catcher. If the game was played in a schoolyard, no catcher was needed because the pitcher threw the ball to a box that was drawn on the wall. That box was the strike zone. If the pitch was within the box, it was called a strike; if not, it was a ball. If stickball was played in the street, there was no wall, and a catcher was needed. The catcher served as both the "wall" (he stopped the ball) and the umpire, who called the pitch a ball or a strike, if the hitter did not swing. The hitter could walk, strike out, or hit the ball into the field of play. When a ball was hit, if it was fielded cleanly (the fielder caught the ground ball or fly ball/pop up), the hitter was out. If the ball got by the fielder, the hitter was awarded at least a single. The batter was awarded a double, triple, or home run, depending on how far the ball traveled on a fly.

When the game was played in the street, the distance the ball traveled (and subsequently the yardstick used for awarding a single, double, triple, or home run) was determined by the street sewers. The round sewer (or manhole) covers served as the measuring stick. The sewers were located in the middle of the street. A sewer also served as home plate. If you hit the ball to the next sewer, you got a single or double, depending on how far apart the sewers were in your neighborhood. If you were a two-sewer man, in many neighborhoods you were awarded a home run. Three-sewer men were envied across every borough in New York City. Willie Mays was a four-sewer man.

We were lucky enough to have a park right across the street from our building, so we didn't have to play stickball in the streets and dodge the cars. The park was extremely dangerous at night but was relatively safe during the day. There were three full-length basketball courts all right next to each other. Our stickball field of play was composed of the width of all three basketball courts. Of course kids playing basketball were not too happy to see batted balls flying past them. In fact, yelling matches were fairly common concerning who had to leave and who got to stay, the stickball players or the basketball players.

Beyond the basketball courts were handball courts with an exceedingly high chain-link fence separating them from the basketball courts. In our park the stickball hitter stood at one end of the basketball courts. A home run was a fly ball that traversed the three basketball courts and went over the fence into the handball courts.

All that was needed to play stickball was a broom handle and a rubber ball, called a Spaldeen. The term, Spaldeen, was New York lingo for the make of the rubber ball, Spalding, which was printed right on the face of the ball. If we wanted balls that would bounce even higher than Spaldeens, we sometimes used Pensy Pinkies. Both Spaldeens and Pensy Pinkies were similar to tennis balls, but without the fuzzy tennis-ball cover. Most of the other groups of kids who played stickball broke the handles off of their mother's broom sticks to use as stickball bats, but even though we never had much money, my friends and I bought stickball bats. They were $1.25, and our stickball bats were thicker than broom handles and had a roll of black tape across the bottoms for a better grip.

The American League had expanded from eight to ten teams in 1961 by adding the newly created Los Angeles Angels and the Washington Senators. Consequently, American League owners extended the season from 154 games to 162. Because Roger Maris had eight more games in which to break the Babe's record, urban legend had it that an asterisk (*) was used to distinguish Maris's record. Some of the kids in the other buildings in the projects, jealous of Billy's record, suggested he deserved an asterisk for using the store-bought stickball bats, rather than the homemade broom-handle ones. However, to this day I still have the record book, and there's no asterisk beside Billy's name. I made sure of it!

Billy Epstein was an unlikely stickball home-run champion. The Linden Projects were formed in June 1958, and many of us moved into our apartments in early 1959. When spring came in 1959, most of the kids my age went outside to play ball, and that's how we met each other. Some of the friendships that started there lasted a lifetime. Freddy Cohen, Ira Stolzenberg, Steve Weiner, and I were the first set of friends that formed, and we would play punchball, stickball, or some other game almost every day. One day Ira told us that there was another kid in his building, 570 Stanley Avenue.

"Who?" I asked.

"His name is Billy," said Ira

"Why doesn't he come out to play?" I asked.

"I'm not sure, but I think he stays inside all the time and reads," said Ira.

"What does he read?"

"I think he reads encyclopedias."

"Stop joking around."

"I'm not joking," said Ira.

That was all we needed to know. The next day we went to Billy's apartment to call on him. He was, indeed, reading encyclopedias, but we finally convinced him to come outside and play ball with us. From that day on Billy Epstein became a fixture in our group. Billy hadn't gotten very far in his encyclopedia reading and was still only in the middle of the A's, but, from that point on, if any of us ever needed to know anything about aardvarks, Billy could tell us all about them.

Chapter 4

YOUR PERMANENT RECORD

*T*he second set of friends that I had were my junior high school buddies. In New York City, at that time in the late 1950s, the city school system offered SP classes. SP stood for Special Progress, and kids in the SP classes condensed the three years it normally took to graduate junior high into two years. My SP buddies and I essentially skipped eighth grade. Supposedly the SP classes were composed of the kids who had the highest IQs in the city. For our first year in junior high, traditional classes were numbered from 7-1 to 7-25, but SP classes were numbered only 7SP1 through 7SP4. There were only four SP classes, compared to twenty-five regular classes. While the regular classes progressed to 8-1 through 8-25 the following year and then finally to 9-1 through 9-25, the SP classes went from 7SP1 through 7SP4 and then straight to 9SP1 through 9SP4.

Even though the SP classes were the cream of the crop intellectually, the regularly numbered classes also had a pecking order. The ones (7-1, 8-1, and 9-1) were composed of the smartest kids who didn't qualify for SP classes. The twos were next-to-the-smartest, and on down. One of my friends was in 7-18. He was pretty bummed out about being in an upper-teens class, because he perceived he was in a class with the dumb kids. When I told him that it could be worse and that he could be in 7-25, he reminded me that classes in the twenties were reserved for the criminals. We noticed that nobody in those classes ever smiled in their yearbook photos. Rumor had it that the school saved money by choosing not to hire a photographer to take their yearbook photos; they just used their police mug shots, taken of all arrested criminals.

And there were plenty of criminals in my junior high. My friends and I went to Junior High School 166, George Gershwin Junior High School. Gershwin Junior High was located right down the street from 580 Stanley Avenue, my address in the Linden Projects. Luckily school was open only in the daytime, because walking even that one block to school during nighttime hours would have been an extremely dangerous proposition. Gershwin Junior High regularly landed on the state's list of persistently dangerous schools. In fact Gershwin eventually closed its doors in 2015, after periods of poor performance and a continued reputation as an extremely unruly place.

My 7SP and 9SP friends and I were unruly as well, but not in a violent way. My two best SP friends were Barney Davis and Stephen Schwartz, whom we called Boobie (pronounced Buh bee). We teased our classmates unmercifully and had nicknames for most of them. My nickname was Skully, which I still use affectionately to this very day. Even now I give my good friends "Skully privileges", thus allowing them to call me by my junior high nickname.

The smartest kid in class, David, was called The Brainiac.

One of our classmates, Frederick, ran to all the classes and waited outside the room. He always had to be the first one in when the door opened for the next class. Fred's 9SP1 yearbook caption reads: "When this boy hears a gong, he picks up speed and beats the throng." We called him Freddy First.

Even our teachers couldn't escape our nicknames. We called

our science teacher Baldy Kaufman, a nickname I now find very ironic, since I have been completely bald since my 35th birthday.

Our unruliness evidenced itself in harmless pranks (or so we thought) that we would play on our classmates.

One fateful Tuesday we decided to target two of our class-mates with whom we didn't get along. Ronald and Judy were inseparable friends and always walked together in the hallways. One day we sneaked up, walked behind them, extended our arms straight in front of us, and clapped them on their ears with our palms. Even though we didn't clap them very hard, they fell down and cried out as if they had been shot. In the NBA this type of faking is called *flopping*, where a technical foul is assessed on a player who intentionally falls to draw a foul, even though little or no physical contact was made. In hockey a two-minute penalty is called for "taking a dive." Although Ronald and Judy should have been assessed a technical foul or a two-minute penalty, this was, unfortunately, not the NBA nor the NHL. Instead, in George Gershwin Junior High, the foul was clearly on us.

The leader of our group, and the person who orchestrated the clapping was a kid named Larry Tischler. The Tisch was short and stocky, but powerfully built. Everyone was afraid of him, includ-ing us, his good friends, but the Tisch was no match for the dean of boys at Gershwin, Jack "Dutch" Garfinkle. Dean Garfinkle was a giant of a man—six feet, six inches and 250 pounds of chiseled muscle. He had played football in high school and college and supposedly once had a tryout with the New York Football Giants. He was rarely seen but often discussed. When a boy transgressed, he was called to Dutch Garfinkle's office for discipline and was told never to talk about what happened to him there. The com-bination of Dutch Garfinkle's reticence to be seen and the gag order imposed on his "victims" made the dean the most feared person on the planet (for us). Our imagination ran wild. Just what did happen in the dean's office? Everything from paddles to straps to yardsticks to electric shock treatments were punishments rumored to have gone on in that office. Just the mention of the name Dutch Garfinkle sent tremors down everyone's spine.

Wednesday, the day after the clapping, we were sitting in Mr. Flatow's French class, throwing spitballs (wadded up pieces of wet paper shaped in a ball) at each other, when the Tisch was summoned to Dutch Garfinkle's office. Tisch never returned to class. Through the window we could see him leaving the school, visibly shaking. Later that same day, everyone involved in the clapping incident, including Barney, Boobie, and me, were summoned to Dutch Garfinkle's office. We were soaked in sweat by the time we arrived at the dean's office.

"Mr. Tischler gave me your names as the other boys who clapped poor Ronald and Judy," said Dean Garfinkle.

"What?" we thought. "The Tisch would never give us up. He's the toughest kid in the school."

"From now until the time you leave George Gershwin Junior High School, you will each have to carry around Conduct Cards," continued Dutch Garfinkle. "Each time you go to a different class, the Conduct Cards will need to be signed by the teacher of that class, attesting to the fact that you behaved yourselves in class—and you will behave! One transgression, and you will be expelled from Gershwin. These Conduct Cards, and everything from this point on until your graduation, if you make it until graduation, will be on your permanent record," concluded the dean of boys and girls.

As soon as we got home from school that day, Barney, Boobie, and I went over to the Tisch's apartment in the neighboring city projects, the Boulevard Houses.

"What happened?" I said. "Why did you give him our names?"

"I refused to give out any names, but then he tortured me.

The pain was so bad that I had to give you guys up," said a lying Larry Tischler.

"If he tortured you, why isn't there a scratch on you?" asked Barney.

"I'm a really fast healer," said the Tisch.

"And now it's on our permanent record," I said.

"What does that mean?" asked Barney.

"I don't know, but it's bad, really bad," I said. "I think your permanent record follows you everywhere until you die. Everywhere we go, and everything we do, even after school is over, will be on our permanent record. It goes with us to college. When we apply for a job, they'll look at our permanent record and tell us to get lost, because of these Conduct Cards. If the police stop us, they'll have our permanent record. Our girlfriends will be able to see it, and our wives, if anyone will ever marry us after this, will have our permanent record to remind us of how terrible we were. Everyone will hate us, all because of a harmless clap."

"And Ronald and Judy weren't even hurt," Barney reminded us. "They flopped!"

We were all convinced that this permanent record would ruin our lives. When we were little kids, it was the dark that scared us. Later on, it was the boogie man, and then bullies from 7-25. But nothing was as scary as knowing something bad was on our permanent record.

Our parents were called to school and told about the incident and about the Conduct Cards we had to carry around everywhere. Needless to say, my mother wasn't very happy. "You beat up Ronald and Judy?" asked my mother, incredulous. "Robert told me they're really nice kids. What's wrong with you? Robert would never do anything like that. My son Mark, the juvenile delinquent. You know, this will go on your permanent record."

Taking one last shot at me, my mother reminded me, "You never had any common sense!"

"What do you have to say for yourself, young man?" my father finally chimed in.

"They took a dive," I could only say in my very weak defense.

Even now I approach most major business requests with trepidation. When applying for a mortgage, a new credit card, or even just renewing my passport, I always harbor the same fear: that a manager will appear and say, "Mr. Skall, everything looks okay except for one item—your permanent record, which, as you know, follows you around everywhere you go. Your permanent record indicates that in 1960 you clapped poor Ronald's and Judy's ears. This incident was obviously profoundly serious, because you received the harshest of all junior high school punishments: the dreaded Conduct Card. Request denied!"

Chapter 5

WHERE THE GIRLS ARE

*F*ollowing my junior high school years, I spent three years at Stuyvesant High School and four years at Brooklyn College. More importantly, whenever I wasn't in school I continued to hang out, as much as I could, with my Linden Project friends. Almost none of my friends from the Linden Projects went to Stuyvesant. In fact I have no idea how I got there. Stuyvesant was established as an all-boys school in 1904. An entrance exam was mandated for all applicants in 1934. I vaguely remember taking the test to get into Stuyvesant, but I'm sure that I had no expectation of passing the test and getting into the school. Even though I had gotten into the SP classes at Gershwin, getting into Stuyvesant was another matter. Most of my friends got into the SP classes, but only a tiny percentage of students across the city qualified to get into Stuyvesant. Out of thirty thousand junior high school students who took the test for Stuyvesant, only about nine hundred were accepted. "Only geniuses got into Stuyvesant," I remember thinking.

Thus when I found out that I had passed the test, I was extremely surprised. I then had to make the first agonizing decision of my life: do I go to Stuyvesant, one of the best high schools in the country, and abandon my friends from the projects or do I go to Jefferson High School, a mediocre school, but one where I could continue to hang out with my best buds from the projects? The fact that Stuyvesant was an all-boys school and didn't become coed until 1969, two years after I graduated, was not something I considered in making my decision. Perhaps I should have.

My parents, of course, wanted me to go to Stuyvesant, but I was leaning toward going to Jefferson. I really didn't want to travel by subway to Manhattan every day and make a whole new set of friends in high school. The BMT subway line, which I would need to use to go to Stuyvesant, was at least a mile from my house, and I would have to walk to the subway station. The thought of walking a mile, perhaps in the rain and snow, and then traveling another forty-five minutes on the subway to get to school really made me think. I took a couple of test runs, walking the mile or so to the BMT subway line and then taking the train to Manhattan to get to the subway stop for Stuyvesant.

New York City subways were very crowded, especially in the morning during rush hour, and the stop for Stuyvesant was only two stops before Union Square/14th Street, where just about everyone else got off. Thus the train was completely full at the stop for Stuyvesant, with no one but a few students getting off. To get off the train there, it was necessary to push through a mass of people who refused to move an inch. In making my trial runs, I was barely able to push through the crowd to get off the train before the doors closed. One time I didn't make it off the train in time and had to go to the next stop and walk back to the school. All these trial runs were reinforcing my gut feeling that I should stay with my Linden project friends and go to Jefferson.

Then I found out that two of my friends from 9SP1 in Gershwin had gotten into Stuyvesant and were planning to go there. Although they weren't from the Linden projects, Barney Davis and Boobie were two friends with whom I had a lot in common. Finding out that a couple of my junior high buddies would be with me in Stuyvesant convinced me to change my mind. As an added bonus, Barney and Boobie were both very good athletes, and it didn't go unnoticed by me that I could ride with them on the subway and use them as my blocking backs to get off at the BMT train stop for Stuyvesant. In fact that's exactly what ended up happening. Barney and Boobie took great pride in knocking reluctant passengers to the side in order to form a big hole for us to run through to get off the train. We were successful all but once, in three years, in getting off the train at the correct stop.

My education at Stuyvesant was superlative, but my social life was nonexistent. Of course I made a lot of new friends and played intramural basketball, baseball, and volleyball with them, but hanging out with only boys at such a formative time of my life was just not natural. I should have been accustomed to it, because in the Linden projects, neither I nor any of my friends had any female friends. We literally didn't know any of the hundreds of girls our age who lived there. We were too busy playing ball.

This was the '60s, the era of drugs, sex, and rock and roll. But my friends and I missed out on two of those three. We listened to every rock and roll song that came out and could name all the songs and all the artists, but sex and drugs were foreign to us. We needed girls for sex, but we didn't know any. And we just never thought about drugs.

At night during the week, most of us stayed in our apartments to study or watch television, but on Friday and Saturday nights, our social life consisted of hanging out on the benches in front of 570 Stanley Avenue and 580 Stanley Avenue. And what did we do on those benches? We talked sports and rock and roll and played telephone. Telephone is a game where we whispered something to the person next to us on the bench; he whispered the same thing to the person next to him, and so on down the line. We then compared the original whispered words to the final words, and they were usually nothing alike. This amused us greatly. That's right. When other teenagers were drinking beer, smoking pot, and getting laid, we were sitting on the benches in front of our buildings playing telephone!

Just about every Stuyvesant graduate went to college; the only question was which college they would go to. I knew then that unless I received a full scholarship, I would be going to one of the free city colleges of New York. Neither my parents nor any of my friends' parents could afford to send their kids to any college where tuition had to be paid. People in the city projects had absolutely no discretionary spending money; thus we knew that we had to qualify for one of the free city colleges or we wouldn't go to college, and qualifying for any of the free city colleges wasn't exactly a cake walk. Talk about pressure!

CUNY (The City University of New York) consisted of a set of free New York City colleges scattered throughout the five boroughs. In the 1960s, before CUNY went to an open enrollment policy in 1970, the city colleges were considered very prestigious and were difficult to get into. One needed a specific high school average and high SAT scores to qualify for one of the free city colleges. These free city colleges had a pecking order at that time, and the high school average needed to qualify for a particular city university reflected that pecking order.

Brooklyn College was the most difficult city college to get into, requiring high school grades in the 90s to qualify. City College was second, requiring grades in the high 80s. I qualified for Brooklyn College, and in 1963 I graduated Stuyvesant and began my college journey at Brooklyn College. In Brooklyn College I was able to be reunited with many of my neighborhood friends who had attended Jefferson. Billy and Ira as well as other

Linden Project friends went to Brooklyn College, but Freddie went to City College.

Even though Brooklyn College was coed, I still continued to avoid associating with girls there. I guess I had gotten so used to hanging around with only boys in high school that my friends in Brooklyn College were, again, all males. I had no clue how to approach a girl or what to say to her. It would be a few more years before I would be comfortable in the presence of girls and learn how to approach them.

Brooklyn College had fraternities and sororities, as well as a concept called house plans. House plans were similar to fraternities, except on a much smaller scale, and they were very popular in the 1960s at Brooklyn College. They were also dramatically less expensive to join. No one I knew was in a fraternity or sorority at Brooklyn College. Clearly, I didn't know anyone in a sorority because I didn't know any girls. But I knew lots of guys, and they were almost all in house plans. In my mind, fraternities were for the rich, stuck-up guys, but house plans were for the average Joes, like kids from the projects.

A few of my friends and I attended a few of the house plans parties to decide whether to "rush" (apply for submission to) the house plan, but then Billy, Ira, and I came up with a novel idea. Why not form our own house plan, just for our tight-knit group from the projects? Furthermore, why not make it an intercollegiate house plan, open to students at other colleges besides Brooklyn College? This plan would allow our dear friend, Freddy Cohen, who was attending City College, and perhaps other kids from the projects attending other city colleges to join. Thus Emanon (*no name* spelled backwards) House was formed.

We went through the laborious task of finding a suitable house to rent near Brooklyn College and even bought a pool table to put in the basement of our rented house that would serve as the headquarters for Emanon House. We also elected the Emanon House officers. Billy was the president, Ira the vice president, and I was the social director. Anyone watching me trying to set up parties and invite girls to attend was in for quite a sight. A social director who literally knew no girls and felt awkward just talking to girls was worth the price of admission alone. Suffice it to say that Friday and Saturday nights were usually spent playing pool among ourselves and waiting for the girls, who invariably were very few or nonexistent, to arrive.

Chapter 6

LADY DI

Gradually and painfully I learned how to approach, and talk to, girls. I had a few dates, and even had one or two girl-friends, if you call three dates with the same girl having a girl-friend. Then on October 31, 1963, Steve Weiner, another one of my friends from the Linden Projects, set me up on a blind date for Halloween with his girlfriend's best friend. My date's name was Diana Rossman, and she was the most beautiful girl I had ever seen. Considering that up to that point my track re-cord with girls had been dismal, I clearly felt like I had just hit a home run. (I really could have used that home run in 1962 to tie Billy for the stickball home run championship.) Diana had brownish blond hair and wore it short like Princess Diana later did. In fact Diana bore more than a passing resemblance to the princess. When Princess Diana joined the British royal family in the early 1980s, most of our friends and I nicknamed my Diana "Lady Di."

Now, there were a few peculiarities about Diana. First of all, she told me her name was Diane, rather than Diana, her real name. (It stuck and it took me more than twenty years to re-learn her correct name.) Second, she told me she loved to play tennis, and third, she told me that Cousin Brucie (a famous rock and roll radio disc jockey in New York) was really her cousin. None of those things turned out to be true. Of course I wasn't so perfect myself, with the exception of my hair.

When I was young, I had the most perfect head of hair you could imagine. My hairstyle was called a DA (short for duck's ass), which consisted of slicked back hair on both sides that met in the back of the head. The edge of a comb was then used to define a central part running from the crown to the nape at the back of the head, resembling the rear end of a duck. To achieve a perfect DA, the hair had to be heavily greased, either with pomade, or, in my case, Vaseline Petroleum Jelly. After combing the greased hair on both sides back, I used my comb to tease the front of the hair out, forming a mini pompadour. I was told that I looked like the popular rock and roll singers of the '60's: Frankie Avalon, Ricky Nelson, and Fabian. I received numerous compliments on my looks.

"Mark is so handsome," my aunts used to say. (My mother, of course, thought Robert was more handsome.) However, I was convinced then and still am, that really nice hair makes up for a myriad of other issues. I was an average-looking guy with incredible hair. Ironically, at the age of 35, I started losing my hair. To this day I still look in the mirror every day when I get up, hoping to see my beautiful hair, but all that stares back at me is my chrome dome. And every day I realize that my junior high days of the '60s aren't coming back, and neither is my hair.

Diana and I were married at Leonard's of Great Neck on Long Island on November 19, 1967. Leonard's was a wedding machine where couples could, as we did, have both their wedding ceremony and reception. Leonard's married Jews, Christians, Mormons, and all other denominations. The sanctuary was multipurpose. Crosses were on the wall for Christian weddings, only to be replaced by Stars of David for Jewish weddings. Chandeliers, marble floors, golden fireplaces, and mirrors were everywhere.

On our wedding day my parents walked me down the aisle before Diana made her entrance, and it was an entrance to behold. She was behind a large curtain, and when the curtains opened, all that could be seen at first was an empty round stage. Then the stage turned, like a lazy Susan, and Diana was transported from the back of the stage to the front, rivaling the glamour and glitz of Las Vegas. Diana then walked off the stage to meet me at the wedding canopy, called the chuppah. At the end of a Jewish wedding ceremony it is customary for the groom to step on and break a glass. The breaking of the glass symbolizes the destruction of the Jewish Temple in Jerusalem. This tradition is included in the Jewish wedding ceremony to symbolize the absolute finality of the marital covenant. Being obsessive-compulsive, even then, I practiced the act of stepping on the glass for weeks prior to the wedding, making sure to break it, all to no avail. Uncle Max (the same one who made my brother Robert into a singing star) performed the wedding ceremony.

Right after Uncle Max proclaimed, "I now pronounce you man and wife," I raised my leg to break the glass.

"After all that practice, this will be a piece of cake," I thought, but it was not to be. I raised my foot and stomped down hard, only to realize that I had missed the glass. I tried it again, and this time caught the edge of the glass and sent the glass rolling away from us. Now I became really determined. On the third try I stomped down hard again and this time shattered the glass, but because of the force of my stomp, I fell to the floor. I casually picked myself up and acted like nothing had happened.

For our honeymoon, while other couples went to one of the Caribbean islands or to Europe, we went to the Catskill Mountains and stayed at the Nevele Hotel, a high-rise resort just outside of Ellenville, New York. Nothing was too good for Lady Di! The Nevele dated back to the Borscht Belt-era of the Catskills, having opened in 1903. Nevele is *eleven* spelled backwards and is rumored to have been named after the eleven schoolteachers who discovered a waterfall within its property.

I must have a thing for backwards names, first starting with Emanon (no name spelled backwards) House and then staying at the Nevele Hotel on our honeymoon. Come to think of it, in junior high my friends and I used to write everyone's names backwards. Besides sounding like a laxative, Kram Llaks was my name spelled backwards.

In addition to the backwards name, what attracted me to the Nevele was that its host was Joe Pepitone, the first baseman for the New York Yankees. Although I was a dyed-in-the wool New York Mets fan, getting to meet a professional baseball player was very appealing to me. Joe Pepitone was a very charming and gracious host, welcoming all the residents to the shows every night and mingling with us on the dance floor. But the icing on the cake was when, on the Wednesday evening after we arrived, Joe said that he was going to introduce a special guest the following night.

When Thursday arrived, right after the show, Joe stepped to the microphone and said, "Ladies and gentlemen, I'd like to introduce your MVP, (Most Valuable Player), Carl Yastrzemski."

I was awestruck. Yaz, as he was known, had just single-handedly carried the Red Sox on his back to an American League pennant and World Series appearance. His 1967 season was arguably the most spectacular season by any hitter since the great Ted Williams. Besides winning the MVP award, he earned a Gold Glove award for his defense and became one of only ten hitters in baseball history to win the Triple Crown by leading the league in batting average, home runs, and runs batted in, a truly spectacular feat. As a huge sports fan, meeting the reigning MVP of the American League, and a player who had just had one of the greatest seasons in baseball history, was huge.

Joe asked the audience if we had any questions for the reigning MVP. I had only one question that had been intriguing me ever since I checked into Yaz's lifetime statistics. I noticed that before 1967, Yaz was always a very good hitter, but had hit very few home runs. He was averaging 15.8 home runs per year and his high, for any year, was 20 home runs. In 1967 Yaz hit 44 home runs! He would later go on to hit 40 home runs two more times, in subsequent years. I can remember my question clearly, as if I asked it yesterday. "Yaz, you've always been a very good hitter, but you've always hit very few home runs until this year," I said. "What accounted for the huge increase in home runs?"

"Well, I've been working out with weights and with my personal trainer. The result has been that my upper-body strength is vastly improved," Yaz answered.

I accepted this answer without giving it much thought. Later, in the 1970s, Tom House, a former major league pitcher, acknowledged that six or seven players per team were experimenting with steroids. By the 1990s steroids had reached epidemic proportions when Bobby Bonds, Mark McGwire, and Sammy Sosa were linked to steroids. Since that time, some very famous hitters have admitted to steroid use. The one thing all these hitters have in common is that their home run totals increased dramatically from their previous norms. I started wondering, "Could Yaz have started the steroid craze well before I even had ever heard of the word *steroids*?" Probably not. The answer Yaz gave may have really been the reason for his meteoric rise in home runs. Then again, maybe my innocent question revealed the true genesis of the steroid era in baseball.

As our honeymoon week neared its end, we were sitting at the Nevele dinner table with other honeymoon couples we had met. We all decided to go around the table for each of us to talk about our future plans and where we would begin our new married lives. Various couples talked about moving to Brooklyn, New Jersey, Staten Island, and Long Island.

When our turn came to enthusiastically discuss where we would begin our married journey, Diana's face turned sad and she said, while holding back tears, "We're moving to Maryland." She then broke down and sobbed uncontrollably.

Chapter 7

LOCATION, LOCATION, LOCATION

*T*he day after our honeymoon ended, Diana and I drove to Maryland to begin our new life. In 1967 we were smack dab in the middle of the Vietnam War, a war I did not support.

Vietnam is a nation in Southeast Asia, and the Vietnam War was a long, costly, and divisive undeclared war that took place in Vietnam, Laos, and Cambodia and lasted from 1955 until 1975. The war pitted the communist government of North Vietnam against South Vietnam and its principal ally, the United States. The United States involvement in the war was driven by the Domino Theory, which posited that one Southeast Asia country falling to communism would result in many other countries following suit. By November 1967, when Diana and I got married, the number of Americans in Vietnam numbered 500,000, and more than 15,000 Americans had been killed. Another 110,000 more were wounded. By the time the war had ended, more than three million people worldwide would be killed, as well as 58,000 Americans.

I did not want to be one of the 58,000. Just the month before we were married, in October 1967, I joined more than 35,000 demonstrators outside the Pentagon, protesting the Vietnam War. My combination of moral outrage as well as a healthy fear of armed combat led me to pursue various mechanisms to avoid being drafted to serve, in my opinion, in a wholly amoral war.

Many of my friends were talking about moving to Canada to escape the draft. My family and I had traveled to Canada on numerous occasions for different family vacations, and I had a very high opinion of the cities in Canada that I had seen: Montreal, Toronto, and Quebec City. They were all beautiful cities with growing economies. However, Canada was missing three things that I could not live without: Major League Baseball, the National Football League (NFL), and the National Basketball Association (NBA). At that time, I was a fanatic New York Mets, New York Football Giants, and New York Knicks fan. In fact to this day, although I can barely remember what I ate for breakfast this morning, I can recite, in excruciating detail, almost any statistic from the New York Mets first year of existence in 1962, including the starting lineup for their first game ever played on April 11, 1962. I could not fathom living in a place where I could not watch professional baseball, football, or basketball.

After I crossed moving to Canada off my list of ways to avoid the Vietnam War, there were still some possibilities left. The selective service had different designations to denote one's eligibility to be drafted, ranging from 1-A (eligible to be drafted) all the way up to 4-F (not qualified for military service, typically because of medical issues). While I was in college I was classified as 2-S, which was a student deferment. Knowing that my 2-S classification would come to end when I graduated from Brooklyn College, I researched all the other possible deferments that I might be able to obtain after graduation.

The most widely discussed classification among my friends and in the newspapers was 4-F. The designation of 4-F started way back in the Civil War. Back then, in order to properly load a rifle quickly, the gun powder needed to be ripped open with one's teeth. Only the incisors and canine teeth in the front could be used for this task. Routine dental care did not exist around the time of the Civil war, and many men were missing several teeth. Dentists examined prospective inductees to evaluate their front teeth or lack thereof, and men without four front teeth were disqualified and designated as 4-F (lacks four front teeth). However, during the Vietnam War, I had heard about many men being given a 4-F designation, and they all had great-looking teeth!

Many of the 4-Fs given out were because of flat feet. "Flat feet" had replaced "lacks four front teeth" as the silliest reason to avoid a war. Flat feet is a non-symptomatic deformity in which the arches of the foot collapse, causing the entire sole of the foot to come into complete contact with the ground. The arch is apparently a great shape to absorb impact. The thinking was that one needed an arched foot to march, run, and carry heavy loads over long distances without wearing down. That thinking seemed nonsensical to me then and still does now, considering that many great athletes in all sports have flat feet. In fact, 12 percent of players in the NBA, arguably the world's most demanding sport, have flat feet, including Hall of Famer Patrick Ewing and near-certain Hall of Famers Tim Duncan, Dwayne Wade, and the late Kobe Bryant. There are players in all the other professional sports, including baseball, football, and hockey, who have flat feet, and thus would have been disqualified from serving in the Vietnam War. Interestingly enough, many hockey players in the National Hockey League do not have their front teeth, so they certainly would have been disqualified from serving in the army during the Civil War. In any case, I ran out and got my feet checked, but alas, they were not flat. Strike one; the 4-F designation was out for me.

Although 4-F was out for me, there were still quite a few other designations that seemed obtainable: 1-AO, and 1-O (both variations of conscientious objector status); 1-D (qualified member of a reserve component); 2-A (occupational deferment); or 3-A (hardship deferment including registrant with child).

The 1-AO classification meant that you were morally opposed to serving in combat, while a classification of 1-O meant that you were morally opposed to serving the military in any capacity. Men classified as 1-AO would be assigned to military service not involving combat, while men classified as 1-O would serve in an alternative service program, such as health care or education. Both conscientious objector statuses, 1-AO as well as 1-O, were classifications that I considered. However, there was a catch. To be a conscientious objector, a person had to demonstrate that he was opposed to the war on religious, moral, or ethical grounds, rather than on political beliefs. One must be opposed to all wars, not a specific war. I was just opposed to the war in Vietnam. Strike two; conscientious objector status was out for me too.

Up until 1965 there was another way to avoid being drafted into the Vietnam War, and it was exceedingly simple to obtain: just get married. Yep, until August 25, 1965, getting hitched was a Get Out of Vietnam Free Card; however, on August 26, Lyndon Johnson signed Executive Order 11241, eliminating this marriage exception to the draft but grandfathering in those already married. The signing of the executive order still gave men until midnight to get hitched; however, most counties on the East Coast, especially in New York, required a "cooling-off" period between getting a marriage license and actually doing the deed.

One exception to this cooling-off period was in a town called Elkton, Maryland, only about a three-hour drive from New York City. Elkton, Maryland became one of the most popular cities in the United States on August 26, 1965, as thousands of couples from all over the East Coast drove there to take their matrimonial vows. Although I wasn't officially engaged in 1965, Diana and I assumed that we would eventually be getting married. Thus we fleetingly considered running off to Maryland (to where, coincidentally, we would eventually move to in 1967) to get married, but still needing to finish my college education and without a job, we finally came to our senses and continued on with our lives as single people.

However, knowing that we would be getting married shortly after graduation from college in June 1967, a related exemption, 3-A, hardship deferment including registrant with child, was something we had to consider. Again, just like in 1965, during 1966 and the early part of 1967, when I was considering this option, I still didn't have a job, not to mention that we weren't even married yet, so having a child really did seem to be putting the cart before the horse. Strike three; no 3-A deferment. I had struck out.

Or had I?

Going back to the drawing board, I continued to scour through the set of Selective Service classifications when I rediscovered the 2-A classification, occupational deferment. That one could really work. From that moment on I approached every job interview with this 2-A deferment in mind. Government agencies that were part of the Department of Defense (DOD) and DOD contractors were my primary targets. However, realizing that New York City was not exactly a hotbed for federal government agencies or DOD contractors, I slowly started to realize that I might have to move away from New York City, my birthplace, and a city that I cherished, to obtain an occupational deferment. However, living hundreds of miles away from my beloved Mets, Giants, and Knicks was far better than fighting an unjust war thousands of miles from there, I rationalized. At least in the U.S. I could check scores of my beloved teams and read some articles on them in the newspapers. I doubted that there would be newspapers to read in Vietnam, and besides, I surmised, I'd be pretty busy fighting.

Shortly after stumbling onto this plan, I was able to land an interview with Grumman Aerospace on Long Island, a major

DOD contractor. This was my big chance to get a draft-deferred job and also stay in New York City. Grumman had set up an elaborate tour for me, scheduled to last all day, which included meeting with the top people there, watching demonstrations of many of their products, meeting with some rank-and-file employees, eating a fancy lunch, and finally participating in one-on-one interviews with several top managers who had expressed a strong interest in wanting to hire me. If I took this job, I could stay in New York and continue to watch the Mets, Giants, and Knicks. Grumman Aerospace seemed to be my ideal job, but there was one thing missing. I had no clue as to whether or not this job would result in a draft deferment. Some DOD contractors were authorized to offer occupational deferments and some were not.

During the initial meeting first thing in the morning, my host excitedly informed me of Grumman's plans to convince me that Grumman was the place for me. "Are there any questions before we begin?" my host asked.

"I have only one question," I said. "Has Grumman been successful in convincing the Selective Service System to grant its employees an occupational deferment?"

"Well, no it hasn't."

"Thank you very much, but Grumman is not the place for me," I sadly countered.

"But we set up a whole day's worth of activities, and we have so many exciting things to tell you. You'll love it here."

"Yes, I may love it at Grumman, but I won't love being in Vietnam a year from now and dying for a bogus cause. I have to pass."

Luckily, I did eventually find a draft-deferred job at the David Taylor Model Basin (DTMB) in Bethesda, Maryland. On the fifth day after I reported to this civilian Navy base for duty, which was one week and five days after Diana had broken down and sobbed on the last day of our honeymoon, I received a copy of the letter that DTMB was about to send to my draft board at 44 Court Street in Brooklyn, New York. The letter began "The following employment information is being submitted so that your board may consider granting Mark W Skall, Selective Service No. 50-45-39-507, an occupational deferment." It then went on to describe my duties in glorious detail. I was already smiling even before I read the concluding sentences, which stated "In view of Mr. Skall's education and technical proficiency, coupled with the shortage of qualified personnel, we request that he be granted a 2-A classification. If we lose Mr. Skall's contributions to our program, it will take at least twenty-four months to bring a replacement, if one were available, to Mr. Skall's level of proficiency."

Mind you, it would take two years to replace me, and I had been working for DTMB for only one week! I was so impressed with what I had accomplished in such a short period of time that I marched into my boss's office and immediately asked for a raise.

Chapter 8

YOU GUYS BET ON EVERYTHING!

*n*ow that I had a job, Diana and I needed to find a place to live. At the suggestion of a few friends in Brooklyn College, who were also moving to Maryland, Diana and I, as well as these friends, moved into Congressional Towers in Rockville, Maryland. Congressional Towers seemed too good to be true. It had central air conditioning, three swimming pools, and four tennis courts, and the monthly rental fee was only $135 a month, much cheaper than any apartments we would have been able to find in New York City. Central air conditioning alone was beyond my comprehension. It meant I had finally succeeded in life. I didn't know anybody with central air. In the Linden Projects we had NO air conditioning, central or otherwise. There was a regulation that tenants were not allowed even to put window units in their apartments, because the power grid couldn't support it. During the hot summer days we played ball all day and avoided the ovens that our apartments had become, but at night we'd come back to an incredibly hot and humid apartment, cooling ourselves with large fans and buckets of ice. To this day I believe that air conditioning, which we were finally blessed with, is the greatest invention of all time.

On my first day of work I left to meet with O.D. Haviland, the head of Personnel at DTMB (it would be many more years before the Personnel Department would be known as the more politically correct Department of Human Resources). After meeting with Mr. Haviland for an hour or two, I went to my new office in the Mathematics Lab. I was seated at a desk in a large room that contained eight desks in total. I met the other seven people in the room, one of whom was my new supervisor, Jean Strickland. Jean was the only female in the room, and aside from one older gentleman, Phil Eddy, Jean was the only one who was not in their early twenties.

Jean described my work assignments to me, and everyone else in the room seemed to be busy at work. However, as soon as Jean left the room to attend a meeting, the room came alive. Everyone except Mr. Eddy, began shouting and joking around and started playing catch with what looked like a replica of a whale made of foam. One of the guys "pitched" the whale to another guy, who hit the whale with a ruler, like he was swatting a baseball with a baseball bat. That was my first introduction to whale ball, a game that my fellow recent college grads and I played every time Jean left the room. Our whale ball game was suddenly interrupted when the phone on my desk (I couldn't believe I had my own phone) rang. I had given Diana my work phone number the day before I started my new job. I answered the phone. Diana was on the phone, crying hysterically. I knew she had loved the new apartment and thought she had gotten over having to move to Maryland. I was really surprised to find her crying. "What's wrong?" I asked.

"Coshroshes," is what I heard through her tears.

"What?"

"Cockroaches. They're all over the apartment."

I had lived in New York for twenty-one years in a city project not known for its cleanliness. I lived without air conditioning and in fear of getting mugged. I had often come back at night to find urine in the elevator and occasionally found puke in the stairways. But one thing we never had (I don't know why) was cockroaches. I had to go 250 miles away to my beautiful new place in Maryland with central air, three swimming pools, and four tennis courts, to discover my first cockroach.

Diana called the Congressional Towers rental office and described her nightmare. Staff from the rental office sprayed the apartment to get rid of the cockroaches, and after a few unsuccessful attempts, they were finally able to rid us of those vile creatures. We could now go back to living our dream life in this wonderful apartment complex.

Besides the amenities in Congressional Towers, another factor that made our life wonderful were the many friends we had in Maryland, almost all of whom also worked at DTMB. My best friend at work, and in Congressional Towers, was Stan Willner. Stan had also previously lived in Brooklyn and, believe it or not, had also lived in the Linden Projects. However, he did not live on the same street, Stanley Avenue, as Billy, Freddie, any other of my friends in the projects, or me. Instead, Stan lived on Wortman Avenue and was a member of a rival "gang", if you could call a bunch of Jewish nerds playing stickball and hit the penny "gangs." Our group would occasionally see Stan's "gang" and sometimes would say hi, but we were not especially friendly with them. Our only real association with this "gang" was playing against them in a basketball league sponsored by a local YMHA (Young Men's Hebrew Association) down the street.

However, I got to know Stan a lot better when we both started going to Brooklyn College at the same time. In fact Stan and another friend of mine from Brooklyn College, Seymour Goldstein, were the ones who told me about the draft-deferred job at DTMB in Maryland. Another friend from Brooklyn College, George Gluck, also lived in Congressional Towers and worked at DTMB.

Stan and I, and sometimes George, loved to bet with each other. We'd bet on anything we could think of: how long it would take us to get to work that day, what time it was currently (we weren't allowed to look at our watches), and a dozen other crazy things. One time we even bet on whether the sun would rise the next day. I said it wouldn't, but I got really good odds!

One time, Stan and I were discussing, and arguing, over a Jewish game played at Chanukah, called the dreidel game. A dreidel is a four-sided spinning top. According to many scholars, the dreidel developed from an Irish or English top introduced in Germany known as a "teetotum." Each side of the dreidel bears a letter of the Hebrew alphabet: nun, gimel, hei, and shin. These letters were originally a mnemonic for the rules of a gambling game played with the dreidel. Nun stands for the Yiddish word *nisht* (nothing); gimel stands for *gants* (all); hei stands for *halb* (half); and shin stands for *shtel ayn* (put in).

Clearly these letters provided a clue as to how the dreidel game was played, but Stan and I could not agree about the exact nature of how to gamble and place bets in the game and what the rules were for betting. So what did we do? We ironically bet on what the rules were for betting in the game! There was no internet in the 1960s to look things up and my cherished Encyclopedia Britannica didn't mention dreidels, so we needed to find an authoritative source on this subject to decide who was correct and would thus win our bet. Who better to be that source than an arbitrary Jewish person? Thus we decided to stop the most Jewish-looking person we could find at DTMB and ask him who was correct. We walked up to a fellow named Harvey Stutz. Harvey had a large nose, dark hair, and a dark complexion.

We knew Harvey's name but didn't know anything else about him, so we walked up to Harvey and asked, "Harvey, are you Jewish?"

Harvey, perhaps already aware of our reputation, looked at us with disdain and said, "You guys bet on everything!" From that time on Harvey went on to become one of Stan's and my best friends and also eventually moved to Congressional Towers.

Having quite a few DTMB employees living at Congressional Towers, we decided to form a carpool to get to work. We were all New Yorkers, except for Harvey, who was a Maryland native, and Roger Martin, who was from Iowa. New Yorkers love to play games. What better time to play games than during a boring ride to or from work? Thus we decided to play games in the carpool.

Stan and I invented two games: the Song Game and the Bet Game. The Song Game, patterned after the word game called Ghost, was fun and was played without any money being wagered. The person who went first would say the first word of a song that he knew the words to. The next person would either say the next word of that song, if he knew it, or would challenge the person to name the song that started with that word, if he thought that no song started with that word. This kept going on indefinitely until someone eventually challenged. The person who was challenged had to then name the song and convince the rest of us that all the words up to that point were correct. If he convinced the rest of us that those were the correct words, he won that round of the game. If he didn't convince us, then he lost. The person whose turn it was could at any time ask the preceding player to sing all the words so far, to help him figure out the song. We all had terrible singing voices, so that tactic didn't really help at all. In fact the so-called singing was actually often painful to listen to and often made it almost impossible to discern the correct song.

While the song game was fun, the other game we played, the Bet Game, was deadly serious. Stan and I would jokingly say that the Bet Game was a second source of income for us and would often result in Roger (from Iowa and thus perhaps more trusting than Stan and me) losing his lunch money to one of us almost every day.

The bet game was played with three people. If we had four people, rather than three, in the carpool that day, one person just watched the other three play. Here are the rules: Two people bet with each other on whether or not the third person knew the answer to a question that the other two chose for him. The two bettors agreed, beforehand, what the answer was to the question being posed. Then the two bettors bet on whether the third person would know the answer. A thumbs up meant that the bettor thought the third person knew the answer and a thumbs down meant the bettor thought that the third person did not know the answer.

If one bettor voted thumbs up and the other voted thumbs down, then an automatic bet of a quarter (twenty-five cents) was made. If the votes were the same, either both thumbs up or both thumbs down, one person had to offer the other person 3:2 odds to entice him to bet the other way. The person being offered 3:2 odds had to either accept that bet or give 2:1 odds to the person offering 3:2 odds. The original odds giver then had to accept 2:1 odds or offer 5:2 odds. This went on until either someone accepted the odds being offered or until 20:1 odds were reached, in which case the person being offered 20:1 odds had to accept.

After the final bet was made, the question was then posed to the third person who then answered it to the best of his ability. This answer determined who would win anywhere between twenty-five cents all the way up to five dollars (twenty times twenty-five cents). Although five dollars might not seem like a lot of money now, remember this was 1968, when our annual salary was approximately $7,000 a year. Also keep in mind that at least five rounds of questions and bets were made during the ride to or from work, resulting in as many as ten bets total in one day. What seemed like an awful lot of money to us could be won or lost. It's no wonder that Roger, our friend from Iowa, told us that his grandmother always warned him to watch out for New Yorkers. If Roger had only listened!

Chapter 9

HARVEY OR IS IT PAUL?

*A*fter Harvey Stutz moved to Congressional Towers, he joined our carpool and became the second non-New Yorker in our carpool. Harvey was born and raised in the Washington, D.C./Maryland area. As it turned out, even though Harvey feigned disgust at his mistaken belief that Stan and I were betting on whether Harvey was Jewish, Harvey loved betting as much as Stan and I did. In fact Harvey organized and ran a football pool at work, where many DTMB employees bet, every week, on which team would win each NFL football game. The football pool was open to all employees, and it became extremely popular. At its apex, as many as one hundred people participated in Harvey's pool.

Creating the football pool, distributing the entries to all interested employees, and computing and determining the weekly results required a lot of effort on Harvey's part. Harvey, of course, did all of this work on the football pool while he was at work. Gambling on federal government premises was illegal, and Harvey and all of us participants hid our involvement in the pool. In fact to disguise our identities in case any of us were caught, we used fictitious names. When Harvey distributed the sheets with all our names and our picks, we couldn't be identified in case anyone at the management level tried to find out who participated.

My name was Egg McMuffin, a tribute to the new and delicious breakfast sandwich sold by McDonald's. I was crazy about Egg McMuffins and sometimes even convinced our carpool to let me stop, on the way to work, to run into Mickey D's to buy one. This crazy idea of a breakfast sandwich consisting of an egg with the yolk broken, garnished with a slice of cheese, as well as Canadian bacon, and served open-faced on a toasted and buttered English muffin initiated a whole new area of potential business for the McDonald's franchise. The first Egg McMuffin was served at the Belleville, New Jersey, McDonald's in 1972. Shortly thereafter it was being served nationwide and had quickly become both my favorite food to eat and my football pool alias.

Stan, Harvey, and I all worked in the Mathematics Lab at DTMB, but rather than work with mathematical algorithms, what we actually did was program computers. It was the early days of computers, and the work we did then would be considered elementary today. Rather than program online, like it is done today, everything was done using punch-card machines. The punch-card machines produced program instructions on punched cards, called Hollerith cards. The punched cards were stiff pieces of paper used to contain digital data represented by either the presence or absence of holes in predefined positions. It took hundreds of punched cards to form a computer program. Data for the computer program was also contained on the punched cards. Both the program and data cards were typically handed in to a central facility within the data-processing organization. The program was then executed there, and the punched cards, along with a printout of the output of the computer program, could typically then be picked up the next day.

Even though Harvey worked on computers, he did all the work on the football pool by hand during the workday, and this effort took up a good amount of Harvey's time. One day Harvey had an epiphany. Why not write a program for the football pool, hand it in at the data-processing central facility desk, and check the results the following day? Great idea, right? Well, it was a good idea, but with disastrous results.

Apparently, someone came to pick up their programming job one day and saw a printout with a bunch of crazy names on it and a listing of NFL football games, specifically stating which team was the favorite and which team was the underdog. Ordinarily printouts at this window contained things like submarine and battleship names. NFL football teams seemed grossly out of place, so the person immediately called the DTMB comptroller.

The following day, Harvey was called into the office of Gene Gleissner, the director of the Math Lab. Sitting beside Gene was the comptroller of DTMB, Ralph Levy.

"Mr. Levy tells me that you were using government equipment and government time to run a football pool," said Mr. Gleissner. "Is this true?"

"Well, yes," Harvey replied.

"Do you know how much money you've cost the U.S. government?"

"The way I see it, I saved the government money!" answered Harvey.

"What?"

"By automating the football pool and putting it on the computer, I actually saved DTMB and the federal government a lot of money," Harvey insisted.

"Please explain that reasoning."

"Well, prior to this week, I did the football pool by hand, and it really was a lot of work. I had to collect data from more than one hundred DTMB employees, fill in the team-by-team selections for each entry in the pool, and then, after all the NFL games were over, I had to compute the amount of wins for each person, compare them to all the other entries in the pool, and figure out who had the most wins and thus won the pool. In the case of a tie, I then had to take the tiebreaking games into account in order to break the tie and determine the winner."

"Well, you were a busy young man, weren't you?"

"Yes, and by my calculation it took me about ten hours each week to do all that work."

"Please get to the point."

"Well, my salary is $9200/ year. That comes out to about $177 a week; thus, my hourly wage is $4.42. Add in overhead, which is typically about 2.4 times the wages, and my hourly rate becomes around $10/hour. Since I did all the work on the football pool while I was in the office, it was costing DTMB around $100 every single week. Once I wrote the program for the computer to perform all the work that I did manually and put it on our IBM 7090 computer, the effort I now spend each week is minimal, very close to zero. Thus I've saved the government $100 for this first week and will save it approximately $1500/year over the course of the whole football season."

I thought Harvey's logic was brilliant.

Mr. Gleissner did not. "You're suspended without pay for one month," was Mr. Gleissner's only reply.

As I said earlier, anticipating that Harvey would eventually be caught and disciplined for running the football pool, we all used aliases for our entries into the pool. Mr. Gleissner, seeing all the fictitious names, asked Harvey to provide him the real names of everyone who was in the football pool. Harvey held steadfast and refused to give up the names. To this day I, and probably most of the football pool participants, are very grateful to Harvey for bearing the brunt of the punishment. This refusal on Harvey's part was extremely unselfish and probably impacted the harsh punishment that was doled out to him for what seemed to us to be a trivial transgression. However, all of us knew the real names of all the other entrants in the pool and what their aliases were. From that time forward, whenever any of us would get into an argument with other football pool entrants, many of us would, in jest, threaten to tell Mr. Gleissner the real names of some of the aliases. I cringed every time I heard the words "Egg McMuffin" spoken in the halls.

As it turned out that blow to poor Harvey was just one of many unfortunate events going on in his life. Just a few weeks before this unfortunate incident, Harvey made his wife and both of his kids terribly angry with him. Harvey and his family had a breed of dog called a Shetland sheepdog (sheltie). The sheltie is a breed of herding dog that originated in the Shetland Islands of Scotland. The sheltie's name was Rusty, and he was the darling of his wife and both of Harvey's kids. Shetland sheepdogs have a high level of intelligence. The Shetland sheepdog ranks sixth out of 132 breeds tested in intelligence. Research found that the average sheltie could understand a command in fewer than five repetitions and would obey a command the first time it was given 95 percent of the time or more. However, Rusty must have been absent when intelligence was given out.

Rusty drove Harvey crazy. Shelties are herding dogs, and as they are wont to do, Rusty would run up and down in Harvey's living room chasing its own shadow and barking incessantly. Despite all efforts to change Rusty's behavior, Rusty continued to perform this maddening routine day and night. Harvey was desperate. He really wanted to get rid of that dog. One day he had his chance. As it turned out, Harvey's wife, Rose, and their two kids were going away for the weekend to visit Rose's parents. Harvey seized this opportunity and, believe it or not, gave the dog away to people he knew who lived on a farm in upstate New York. When Harvey's family returned later that weekend, Harvey waited by the door for them to enter and then broke the news. "Can you all please sit down? I have something to tell you."

"Can't I take off my coat?" asked Cheryl, his oldest child.

"This will just take a minute. I gave Rusty away to a nice family in upstate New York. He's in a beautiful home with wonderful people."

"But we're a nice family in a beautiful home," countered Cheryl.

"He's kidding around," said Jason, Harvey's youngest.

"I'm not kidding around. Rusty's on a farm with lots of room to run around. He's very happy."

Perhaps Harvey was unaware of the fact that often when a pet dies, kids, too young to understand are sometimes told that their pet went to a farm. Well, in this case, Rusty literally went to a farm.

As if being suspended for running a football pool and antagonizing his family with the dog incident was not enough misfortune, Harvey was having marital issues and would soon end up getting divorced from Rose. Harvey attributed much of his misfortune, including his divorce, to his name. He just hated the name *Harvey*. He would complain about it to all his friends and thought that the name *Harvey* brought him bad luck.

About a year after the unfortunate incident with the football pool, Harvey showed up at our weekly poker game with some news for us. "I'm changing my name to Paul," said Harvey. Almost everyone sitting around the card table thought he was kidding. I knew he was not.

"That's funny," I countered. "I'm changing my name to Harvey."

For the rest of the card game, whenever anyone addressed a question to Harvey and called him by his current name, Harvey refused to answer. "Call me by my new name, Paul," he would say. Since Harvey refused to answer any questions directed to him using his name, and because I jokingly informed the crew that I was changing my name to Harvey, I, of course, answered in his stead. It was a very confusing card game.

Harvey's friends, including the people at the card game, weren't the only ones who refused to call Harvey by his new name. His wife, soon to become his ex-wife, and his kids also refused to call Harvey by his new name. Eventually, however, Harvey wore us down and we all started calling him Paul. I still know Harvey/Paul today. He lives down the block from me in North Carolina, and to this day, even though everyone calls him Paul, I still have a hard time thinking of him as anyone except Harvey.

Chapter 10

CAN'T ANYBODY HERE PLAY THIS GAME?

E ven though I was young then, I had been a Brooklyn Dodgers fan in the 1950s. By the 1950s, the Brooklyn Dodgers had been a storied franchise in the Big Apple for more than half a century. The team that was to become the Brooklyn Dodgers started life as the Brooklyn Grays in 1883. Nicknames used by fans and sports writers, during their early years included the Atlantics, the Bridegrooms, Brooklyn Ward's Wonders, Superbas, and Robins. In 1895 the team name became the Brooklyn Trolley Dodgers. The Trolley Dodgers played at Eastern Park, near Eastern Parkway, a major boulevard in Brooklyn. The Trolley Dodgers referred to the necessity of pedestrians having to dodge street-level trolley lines, which in 1892 switched from horse-driven trolleys to electrically powered trolleys, making them much more dangerous. *Trolley* was later taken out of its name, and the name Brooklyn Dodgers was finally adopted in 1913.

Like all Dodgers fans, I hated the New York Yankees. And like all Dodgers fans, my heart was broken when our beloved Brooklyn "Bums" abruptly left town and moved to Los Angeles in 1957. Since the New York Giants had also moved to California in 1957, it left New York as a one-team baseball town and that one team, the Yankees, was a team for whom I would never root.

After the Dodgers abandoned our city, I had no rooting interest in baseball until 1962. In 1962 the National League expanded by adding the Houston Colt 45's (later to become the Houston Astros) and the New York Metropolitan Baseball Club (known as the New York Mets). In tribute to the two teams that left the Big Apple for California, the Mets took the colors (blue) from the Dodgers and (orange) from the Giants as their team colors. For the first two years of their existence, the Mets played their home games in the Polo Grounds, the previous home of the Giants, while waiting for their permanent home, Shea Stadium, to be built. After a five-year wait, I finally had a team for whom to root.

And root I did. After I suppressed my baseball hunger during the five-year hiatus of National League baseball in New York, my baseball passions were finally unleashed. I became a fanatical Met fan, going to as many games as I could, and watching almost all of the rest of the games on television.

The Mets lost their first game 11-4 and went on to lose their first nine games. They lost games by one run and by ten runs. I had watched every loss on television. Then on April 23, 1962, I decided to go to the movies with Freddy and Billy, even though the Mets were scheduled to play the Pirates at Forbes Field that night. The Mets were 0-9 and the Pirates were 10-0, so a Mets victory was as probable as a man walking on the moon. Another loss, which would set the record for the most losses to begin a season, was inevitable. When we returned from watching *Journey to the Seventh Planet*, we saw some kids talking excitedly and gesturing. They told us that the Mets had won the game 9-1 and Jay Hook, one of the Mets quintet of terrible starting pitchers, had pitched a complete game. I was upset that I had missed watching this historic occasion, but I was in ecstasy that the Mets had finally won.

To this day I cannot explain what triggered my obsession with the historically awful 1962 Mets, but it was truly an obsession. I knew the life story of every Met player and waited for each player to come out of the clubhouse at the Polo Grounds, after the games I attended, and respond to chants from the crowd by doffing their caps or waving their hands. This devotion was to a team that to this day still has the record for the worst winning percentage in the modern era of major league baseball. In 1962 the Mets won 40 games and lost 120, a .250 winning percentage. Mercifully two games were rained out that year and were never rescheduled.

The Mets were not only my passion in the early 1960s, but they may have actually saved my life. East New York was a very rough neighborhood, and my friends and I were always on the lookout for gangs. Most of us had been stopped previously by gangs. The gangs would typically ask for money, but their real intent was to beat people up. If they asked for a dime and you gave it to them, they would then ask for a quarter. If you gave the quarter to them, they would ask for a dollar, and so on. When you eventually stopped giving them money, they would shove you, punch you, or knock you down.

Although we suspected that many of these gang members had knives (guns were not common in those days in East New York), none of us had been knifed yet. Although we heard that the gangs had knives, we had never actually ever seen anyone carrying a knife. The gangs would almost always outnumber the people they accosted by a ratio of 5:1 or more so they really didn't need a knife to cause havoc. When walking to or from the IRT or BMT subway lines, we would often see groups of unsavory characters hanging around and speaking loudly. We didn't know if they were gangs or just a bunch of jerks. But just to be sure, we would always take the long way home or to the subway, thus ensuring that we did not walk within a block or two of the potential trouble, especially at night.

Although the gangs would typically accost any and all kids as long as they outnumbered them, there was one exception. The East New York gangs had a code of honor. They would leave you alone if you were walking with a girl.

I therefore felt safe one night in May 1963 when I took my girlfriend, Estelle, to the movies on Pitkin Avenue. I had put on my mohair sweater that my Aunt Esther had knitted for me. That sweater was my favorite. The sweater was composed of blue mohair throughout, except for the sleeves, which were knitted in a darker shade of blue. This contrast in material and color made it the coolest sweater I had ever seen. In my mind my new sweater, in combination with my cool-looking hair, made me look like the rock and roll singers I so admired.

Estelle lived near the movies, so my plan was to take the subway to her house and then we would walk from there to the movies. After arriving at Estelle's house, I chatted for a few minutes with her mother. We left Estelle's house, walked a few blocks, and then turned onto Pitkin Avenue toward the movie theater. Estelle was equally impressed by Aunt Esther's sweater and was telling me how handsome I looked in it when a bunch of thugs walked up to us and asked us for money. There were at least seven or eight guys in this gang. I was really surprised, because being with my girl, I didn't understand why these guys did not respect the "code of honor." I then realized that I wasn't in East New York. I quickly surmised that gangs in other parts of Brooklyn must have had different codes. This gang was also different than the ones in East New York in that they all were carrying switchblade knives that were visible and clipped to their belts.

"You got a dime?" said the ringleader, who was wearing a baseball cap backwards.

I didn't answer.

"I said you got a dime?"

"I don't have any money," I replied.

"You don't, huh? Well, we're going to have to search you," replied the ringleader, who then grabbed me by my sweater with one hand, while brandishing his knife with the other.

I reacted instantaneously. I loved that sweater so much that I instinctively and foolishly took his hand, pulled it from the clutches of my sweater, and spun him around.

"Mark, don't hurt him," said Estelle, to my astonishment. She was worried about me hurting him!

I was terrified, but when I spun the ringleader around, I noticed that I could then discern the type of cap he was wearing, and it was a Mets cap. I had to think fast. I remembered that the Mets played later that night. "Listen, we were just going to the movies and then back to my girlfriend's house to watch the Mets game," I lied. I had no intention of watching the Mets game after the movie. Since Estelle was telling me how handsome I was, I figured I could miss one Mets game in order to make out with her.

"You're a Mets fan?" asked the guy who had my life in his hands.

"From day one, man. I can name the whole starting lineup for the first game they ever played."

"Why didn't you say so? Me too! I think Ron Hunt's gonna be rookie of the year. He's a lot better than that Pete Rose guy."

"Yeah, Ron Hunt's gonna be in the Hall of Fame one day, and Pete Rose sucks," I replied, of course willing to agree with anything he said.

"All right. You guys go ahead. You cool, and so is your lady."

I don't know what would have happened if I hadn't noticed the Mets cap on the ringleader's head and told those little white lies. Suffice it to say that I would have, at least, gotten beaten up, probably stabbed, and possibly even become another murder statistic in the Big Apple. By the way, Ron Hunt came in second to Pete Rose in the Rookie of the Year voting that year and became a journeyman second baseman while Pete Rose went on to become one of the greatest players in the history of major league baseball.

I continued to follow the Mets with this same passion throughout the 1960s. The Mets slowly (very slowly) improved throughout the 1960s, but through 1968, the most games they had won in a season was 73, not nearly good enough to have achieved even a .500 record.

Then in 1969 a miracle occurred. The 1969 New York Mets won 100 games and won the new National League East Division title and then defeated the Atlanta Braves to win the National League pennant. They then went on to face the Baltimore Orioles in the World Series. The team that represented the utmost in futility was going to the World Series!

I was elated. However, no one expected them to win the Series. The Orioles won an astounding 109 games in 1969 and were considered one of the greatest teams of all time. Needless to say, the Orioles were a prohibitive favorite over the Mets, who until 1969 had never finished higher than ninth place, next to last.

When the Orioles beat the Mets and their ace pitcher Tom Seaver 4-1 in game one, almost everyone was expecting the Orioles to sweep the Mets in four straight games. One team did, indeed, win four straight games, but it was the Mets, not the Orioles. The Mets went on to win the next four games, after losing the first, thus winning the Word Series in five games. This feat was one that not even the Mets' most ardent supporters, including me, ever imagined. It truly seemed like a miracle. In fact even the manner in which the Mets won this series justified their "Miracle Mets" moniker.

In game four Ron Swoboda, a mediocre fielder at best, made an incredible diving catch of a ball hit by Hall-of-Famer Brooks Robinson to stop an Orioles rally, allowing the Mets to win the game in the tenth inning on an Orioles error by one of the best fielding teams in baseball.

But game five provided a true miracle. This game contained one of the most unusual plays in the history of the World Series. In the bottom of the sixth inning, the Mets were trailing 3-0 when Orioles pitcher Dave McNally appeared to hit Mets' batter, Cleon Jones, on the foot. But the umpire ruled that the ball hit the dirt, rather than Jones. Mets manager Gil Hodges, who ironically played first base for the Mets in the first game of their existence in 1962, got the baseball and showed it to the umpire. The ball had black shoe polish, presumably from hitting Jones's black baseball cleats. Jones was awarded first base and then scored on series MVP Donn Clendenon's home run.

The Mets went on to tie the game in the seventh inning on a home run by Al Weis, of all people. Weis hit only seven home runs in his major league career, and this was the first home run he ever hit at Shea Stadium, where the Mets had been playing since 1964. The Mets then scored the winning runs by tallying twice in the eighth inning, one of the runs scoring on an unusual double error by this usually excellent fielding Orioles team. In 1969, the same year that a man finally walked on the moon, an equally improbable event occurred: the Amazing Mets won the World Series.

"Can't anybody here play this game?" is what the Mets first manager Casey Stengel asked in 1963 after yet another Mets loss. Just a few years later, in 1969, the answer to Casey's question was a resounding "yes!" The Mets went from the worst team of all time to world champs in seven short years. No one could have predicted that. As Yogi Berra said in one of his memorable quotes, "It's tough to make predictions, especially about the future."

Chapter 11

HE LOOKS LIKE MEL TORME!

The improbable feat by the Mets already made 1969 a year I will always remember; however, that year became even more special to me, just a month or so after the World Series ended.

The letter from DTMB in 1967 stating that I was so valuable that it would take two years to replace me did the job of keeping me out of Vietnam. In December 1967, I was awarded a 2-A occupational deferment from the Selective Service System, which was still in effect in 1969. I no longer needed what I once pondered trying to obtain in 1966 and early 1967: a 3-A Selective Service deferment that would have allowed me to avoid being drafted because I had a child. But in the spring of 1969, I discovered that I could have obtained such a deferment. Diana and I found out that we were going to be parents for the first time. We were elated.

In July 1969 we were driving to Washington Hospital Center, where Diana was scheduled to give birth, for blood tests and a routine checkup of Diana and the baby. We were driving in my 1965 red Ford Mustang, my most prized possession.

The Mustang was officially introduced on April 17, 1964. Since April was four months before the normal start of 1965 production, the original Mustangs were often referred to as

1964½ cars but were officially marketed as 1965 cars. When I first saw that sleekly styled car, I knew I had to have one. The selling price of the first Mustang was $2,368.00; however, I still lived in Brooklyn in 1964 and I was a full-time college student. I worked part-time in the summers but could hardly save up enough money to buy my first car for what seemed like such an exorbitant price. I therefore continued to share my dad's boring 1962 Mercury Comet with him, driving it only when my dad didn't need it.

In 1967, as I was planning my wedding and my move to Maryland, I knew I needed to buy a car. A new Mustang was out of the question, but, with my dad's help, I was able to afford a used 1965 red Mustang, my dream car.

The route to Washington Hospital Center took us through crowded D.C. streets, but since I was driving in my most prized possession, I didn't mind, as we turned onto Porter Street. We had driven two or three blocks on Porter Street, when in the flash of an eye, a big Chrysler Plymouth broadsided us and pushed our little Mustang fifty feet off to the side.

I got out of the car and ran to help Diana out. As I exited the car, I couldn't help noticing that the driver's seat really didn't exist anymore, having been replaced by crushed metal from the side of the door that curved over where the driver's seat would have been. Although I ended up with many black and blue marks all over my body, the fact that I escaped serious injury amazes me to this very day.

My once beautiful, shiny red mustang was reduced to an unusable heap of metal. However, my far bigger concern was for the wellbeing of my wife and unborn child. Although the Chrysler had hit my side head on and did not make direct contact with the passenger side where Diana was sitting, the tremendous effect of the crash was still felt by Diana. When an ambulance arrived, I immediately told them that Diana was pregnant, and they quickly put her into the ambulance. I jumped in with her, and we took off for Washington Hospital Center.

As the EMTs led Diana into the hospital, they shouted, "Emergency: pregnant woman." A doctor ran up to us and said, "Ma'am, when did the contractions start?"

"I'm not giving birth," replied my wife, indignantly. "I'm only four months pregnant. Do I look big enough to be giving birth?"

The doctors checked out Diana and told us that everything seemed to be okay, but that they couldn't be certain until the baby was actually born. The five-month wait between the accident and Diana's eventual delivery was excruciating and seemed to last an eternity.

We were both getting anxious as her due date in November quickly approached. I remember reading that Julius Irving (Dr. J), the greatest basketball player in the world at that time, was going into Washington Hospital Center in the latter part of November 1969 to have minor knee surgery. Since Diana's due date was November 25, I was looking forward to perhaps meeting Dr. J while simultaneously experiencing the exhilarations of becoming a father.

However, that was not to be.

During a mother's pregnancy the baby is surrounded and cushioned by a fluid-filled membranous amniotic sac. When this membrane ruptures (typically called the water breaking), it signals the beginning of labor. On November 11, a full two weeks early, Diana's water broke. While we were driving frantically to the hospital in our new Dodge Coronet, I remember thinking that my son or daughter would now be born before Dr. J would arrive. However, not even the disappointment of missing one of my sports idols could dampen the excitement I felt as we neared the hospital.

We arrived at Washington Hospital Center around two a.m., with towels between Diana's legs to stop the gushing watery fluid from forming a lake in the hospital lobby. Unbelievably, nineteen hours later, at eleven p.m., Diana still hadn't given birth. During this time I had been fed two excellent meals by the hospital staff, which of course did nothing to placate my wife, who was screaming in pain and couldn't eat anything except for ice chips the nurses had given her to suck on. She was not only scared and in pain but also very hungry, because she hadn't eaten all day. The staff was also gracious enough to bring a portable TV into Diana's room, allowing me, sitting on a folding chair next to her bed, to watch a basketball game.

I was absorbed in the Baltimore Bullets basketball game, watching Earl "The Pearl" Monroe make another incredible driving layup, so I was startled when the nurse tapped me on the shoulder to tell me that they were wheeling Diana into the delivery room. Shortly after that, the blessed event occurred. At 11:57, after almost twenty hours of labor, Howard Jay Skall was born and the doctor pronounced him a normal, healthy baby. We breathed a sigh of relief. When the staff cleaned my baby up and wheeled him out, Diana was no longer in pain and was, of course, beaming from ear to ear.

"Who do you think he looks like?" asked Diana. "I think he looks like me, although I think he has your eyes," she added.

I didn't say anything.

"Who do you think he looks like?" Diana repeated.

"Mel Torme," I answered.

"Very funny. Who do you think he looks like?"

"He really does look like Mel Torme," I answered again.

Diana started crying hysterically.

Now, Diana rarely, if ever, cried. The only two other two times I could remember it happening was when she told all the other honeymooners at the Nevele Hotel that we were moving to Maryland and when she discovered cockroaches in our new apartment in Maryland. Apparently, my unbiased opinion that our son looked like a cabaret singer who appealed to our parents' generation set her off. But I couldn't tell a lie. The resemblance to Mel Torme was unmistakable.

Mel Torme was born in 1925, making him ten years younger than my mom and dad, so he was much closer to my parents' age than to our age. He was nicknamed the Velvet Fog and he was a jazz singer, drummer, composer, and arranger. He also acted in radio, film, and television and even authored five books. He composed the music and cowrote the lyrics for "The Christmas Song," which most people identify by the first line, "Chestnuts roasting on an open fire." It is the most performed Christmas song of all time and was made famous by Nat King Cole.

Mel Torme was exceptionally talented and very accomplished in his craft, but none of those facts were known to me on November 11, 1969. Mel Torme was not someone whose music I ever listened to or whose career I followed at all. I'm really not sure how I knew what he looked like, but I did know. And he looked exactly like my newborn son.

The next day many friends visited us at the hospital to see us and the baby.

"He looks just like you," proclaimed our friend Maxine.

"No, I think he looks like Mark," said her husband, Stan.

"You're all crazy," said my mom, who, with my father, had flown up from Florida to see her first grandchild. "He looks like Bernie. He has the same exact mouth."

Diana was elated to hear these comments. No one mentioned that he looked like Mel Torme. Later, right before they left the hospital, I pulled our visitors aside one by one, showed them a picture of Mel Torme, and asked them who this singer from another generation looked like.

"Wow! He looks just like Howard," was the answer most of them gave.

To this day I've never relayed to Diana our visitors' exit conversation. I didn't have the courage to tell Diana that neither our relatives nor our closest friends could deny our newborn baby's uncanny resemblance to the then 44-year-old Mel Torme.

Chapter 12

BRING YOUR OWN KNOBS

a las, Howard's uncanny resemblance to Mel Torme was only temporary. Within a few weeks his features changed, and he then looked like a typical one-month-old baby, indistinguishable from the other one-month-olds. Having a newborn baby did not restrict Diana's and my social life. Even though Diana was no longer working and was an excellent full-time mother to our son, we believed in exposing Howard to babysitters at a very young age. Thus we would still go out and socialize, usually on Saturday nights, typically with friends, some who had children and some who did not.

We were slowly making many new friends in our residence in Rockville, Maryland. We had friends in Congressional Towers, friends I had met at work, and friends I had made playing basketball, tennis, and softball. Our friends were truly diverse. They all had different backgrounds and different interests, but they all seemed to have one thing in common: they were all talking about the new concept called Marriage Encounter, which was a weekend retreat for married couples that had the goal of turning good marriages into great marriages.

Marriage Encounter was all the rage in the late 1960s and early 1970s. However, Marriage Encounter actually started in 1952 by a young priest in Spain who developed seminars for married couples to help them focus on open and honest relationships, primarily through improved communications.

Couples who enrolled in Marriage Encounter spent a weekend at a retreat with other couples learning a new form of communication. Marriage Encounter was initially established by the Christian church but was growing and was embraced by other religions. Our Catholic friends had gone to a Catholic Marriage Encounter, and our Jewish friends had attended Marriage Encounter with a rabbi and other Jewish couples.

Marriage Encounter sounded like fun. What did we have to lose? For a nominal fee we would spend a weekend at a nice hotel and meet other young couples. Even though Diana and I are Jewish, we are not especially religious, and we wondered how we'd feel spending a weekend at an event led by a rabbi, which was sure to stress Judaism and perhaps remind us that we were not very good Jews and did not regularly attend synagogue. Thus, we decided to enroll in the Catholic Marriage Encounter, thinking that we could just ignore the religious aspect of the weekend and concentrate instead on the social and cultural aspect.

We made our plans to attend Marriage Encounter at the Hampshire Motor Inn in Takoma Park, Maryland. Our Marriage Encounter weekend was scheduled for late November in 1970. We were extremely excited about the weekend, and we started asking more detailed and specific questions to our friends who had already attended a Marriage Encounter weekend. We learned a lot about what happens at Marriage Encounter. One thing we found out was that the food provided wasn't particularly good and that there was nowhere to buy snacks.

But the second thing we discovered was almost a showstopper. Our friends explained the Marriage Encounter process. There were general sessions where the host (in this case the priest) teaches the couples the communication technique involved. The technique consisted of couples writing love letters to each other. The couples would then go back to their hotel rooms and practice the technique. We were apparently supposed to write these letters to each other and then discuss the content for a set amount of time.

To encourage couples to write these letters and then discuss the content of the letters, Marriage Encounter wanted as few distractions as was possible. Thus, we found out that Marriage Encounter removed the knobs from the television sets so that the couples could not watch TV and become distracted from their writings and discussion. In those days TVs did not have remote control mechanisms and were operated by manually turning the TV on by pulling one knob and changing the channels by turning another knob. The on/off knob also served as the volume control knob.

Diana and I watched a lot of TV, so that the removal of knobs would ordinarily be an issue, but it was something that we could have sacrificed to make this weekend work. However, what was not subject to sacrifice was my ability to watch football on Sundays. Now that we lived in Maryland, it was difficult for me to watch my New York Giants play on Sundays. Sometimes I would go, with other Giants fans, to a "Giants bar" that televised the games via a satellite dish. This plan sometimes worked and sometimes did not. The bar owners wanted to make as much money as they could, so that as long as the Giants fans came in large numbers, the Giants game would be on their satellite dish. However, occasionally a large group of Giants fans did not show up and a larger contingent of fans from another team (usually the Pittsburgh Steelers) showed up in droves. On those occasions the bar switched the game from the Giants game to the Steelers game to keep the large mass of Steeler fans happy and to keep them ordering beer.

Consequently, the only time I knew for sure that I could watch the Giants game on TV was if they were scheduled to be on the local stations. The Sunday of the scheduled Marriage Encounter weekend was a Sunday when the Giants were not only scheduled to be on local TV, but they were also playing their archrival and the team I loved to hate, the Washington Redskins. Watching a Giants-Redskins game was usually my sports highlight of the year. When I discovered this conflict between attending the Marriage Encounter weekend and watching my beloved Giants on TV, I wasn't quite sure how to resolve it. Then an idea hit me.

"Let's just take the knobs off of our TV at home and bring them with us," I excitedly said to Diana.

"What? Are you crazy?" replied my wife, clearly exasperated.

"Why can't we do that?"

"For one thing, you can't modify the hotel's TV. When they came to make up our room, they would discover that the knobs were missing, and they could kick us out. For another thing, it wouldn't work. I don't think the knobs are interchangeable."

"Well, let's give it a try."

I called up my friend Stan, who was by far the smartest person I knew and as far as I was concerned, one of the smartest people in the world. "Stan, are the knobs on TVs interchangeable?" I asked.

"Well, Mark, that's a strange question," replied my go-to person for all questions. "Why do you ask?"

"I need to take the knobs off of my TV and use them on a TV in a hotel,"

"Don't hotel TVs all come with knobs?"

"Yes, but this hotel is removing its TV knobs before Diana and I check in there."

"I understand," said Stan, clearly not understanding. "My guess is that different TVs have different-sized knobs. Why don't you take the knobs off of your TV and bring them over to my apartment and see if they work on our TV?"

I took the on/off control knob that also controlled the volume, as well as the channel selector knob, off of our TV and went over to Stan's apartment, which was in the neighboring building to ours in Congressional Towers. Stan took the knobs off of his TV and I tried to put our knobs on, but no matter how hard I tried, I could not get them to fit.

"It's not the end of the world," said Stan.

"Pretty close," I replied.

"The solution is obvious. Why don't you find out what type of TVs the hotel has and bring knobs from the same type of TV?"

That made sense. I immediately called up the Hampshire Motor Inn. "What kind of TVs do you have?" I asked.

"We have brand new nineteen-inch color TVs," responded the obviously proud hotel operator.

"But what kind? Who is the manufacturer?"

"I really don't know. Nobody's ever asked that before."

"Can you find out?"

"Hold on, sir." After a pause the operator came back on the phone. "They are RCA TVs, sir. Is that okay with you?"

"I really don't care. Thank you."

I ran home and checked my TV, and it was a Zenith.

Panic set in, and I again called Stan.

"What kind of TV do you have?"

"Let me check." After a short pause he came back on the line. "We have a nineteen-inch RCA."

"Can I use your knobs this weekend?"

"Well, Mark, that's another strange question, but sure, why not? My knobs are your knobs."

"Stan, I could kiss you."

"Pass," was Stan's cryptic reply.

Armed with a suitcase and a bag containing M & M's, pretzels, potato chips, and knobs from Stan's TV, Diana and I checked into the Hampshire Motor Inn on Friday to begin our weekend. After receiving the key from the front desk, we took the elevator to our room on the third floor where we met a young couple also beginning their Marriage Encounter weekend.

The husband, whose name was Jerry, said, "Wow, that's a big bag. I can see that box of pretzels on the top. I guess you also heard they don't serve enough food this weekend."

"That's what we heard," I said.

"We just checked in an hour ago, and the food's the least of our worries. They took the knobs off of the TV! I'm a big Redskins fan, and I wanted to watch the game on Sunday."

"Well, we brought our own knobs. I'm a Giants fan, and there's no way I was gonna miss that game."

"You brought your own knobs?" asked an in incredulous Jerry.

"Yup," I said proudly. "And as you can see, we've also got food for the game. You're welcome to watch the game in our room."

"Thanks! Mind if I invite our friends Rob and Jane as well? They came with us to the weekend, and they're also big Redskins fans."

"We don't mind," I responded, while sneaking a peek at Diana's expression. My wife did not look happy.

Bright and early Saturday morning, Marriage Encounter began. We met the Catholic priest who was not much older than we were. He was genuinely nice and highly informative. He explained to us that we would be writing love letters to each other. For the first round of letters, we would spend thirty minutes writing to each other, each letter on a different subject, and we would then spend thirty minutes discussing the letters. By combining the written with the oral communication, we would learn to be much more effective communicators.

Saturday morning came and went, and we performed two 30/30's, as they were called.

On Saturday afternoon the ante was raised, and we wrote for sixty minutes and then spent sixty minutes discussing the content of the letters.

Sunday was to be the culmination of all of our hard work, the 90/90. On Sunday the couples were to write ninety-minute love letters and then go back to their "knobless" rooms to lovingly discuss their long and passionate love letters. I had been told by other couples who had previously attended Marriage Encounter that one of the probable outcomes of this intense and passionate 90/90 love letter session was for the couples to get very emotional, then very romantic, and then culminate the 90/90 with an intense lovemaking session.

Sunday quickly arrived and Diana and I wrote our love letters. During this 90/90, we could hear the footsteps of the priest walking around the hotel floors, listening to make sure that there were no distractions during the especially important finale. While the priest was making his rounds, Jerry, Rob, and I were gathered around the TV in my room crunching on pretzels and potato chips and watching the Redskins-Giants game. Our wives were sitting on the cheap hotel chairs and fuming. The knobs I had brought with me were used to make the volume low enough so that the game couldn't be heard outside the room but loud enough for us to hear.

For many of the couples the Marriage Encounter Weekend ended with an intense and satisfying emotional discussion followed by passionate sex. For Jerry, Rob, and me, it ended with an intense and satisfying football game and a promise by our wives never to have sex with us ever again!

Chapter 13

TOPLESS IN CANCUN

*T*he Marriage Encounter weekend was a welcome diversion from our routine, but by 1973 we still hadn't had a real vacation since our honeymoon. We had just bought our first home in Olney, Maryland, and with new mortgage payments and the cost of raising our son, we did not have much disposable money for a vacation. However, our neighbor Marsha, across the street from our new house on Darnell Drive, was a travel agent, and she suggested that there were many cheap vacations if you booked them at the last minute.

We were talking to Marsha one cold February morning. "Man, it's cold," I said. "I would love to go somewhere warm. Plus, we haven't been on a real vacation in years."

"How about Cancun?" asked Marsha. "We have some great deals for Cancun if you can leave within a week."

Diana and I looked at each other and at almost exactly the same time, replied "Yes!"

We called up my parents, and they agreed to come up from Florida to stay with Howard.

A week later we were off to Cancun. We arrived at the airport and were transported via a shuttle to our hotel. The hotel was a bit shabby and was not on the beach, but it was only a short taxi ride from the beautiful Caribbean Sea surrounded by many beautiful beaches. Our hotel did have a nice pool, and right after our arrival, we were soaking up the sun on one of the lounges by the pool. We were discussing how cold it was in Maryland when the couple next to us heard our discussion.

"Are you from Maryland?" asked the young woman, whose name we learned later was Abby.

"We sure are," I answered.

'Where do you live?"

"We just moved to a small town called Olney," Diana answered.

"What a small world," Abby replied. "We live in Aspen Hill. That's only about fifteen minutes from you."

For the rest of the week in Cancun, Diana and I and Abby and her husband, Larry, were inseparable. We went to dinner with them, shared taxis to the beach with them, and spent almost all of the next couple of days talking and swimming in the ocean with Abby and Larry. On Wednesday, after we'd been in Cancun for three days, the four of us decided to have drinks and dinner at one of the fancy hotels located right on the beach.

Larry and I took a taxi to the fancy hotel in the late afternoon. The plan was for us guys to have a few drinks at the hotel while the wives went shopping. The girls would meet up with us at around dinnertime.

Larry and I started drinking shots of tequila at the bar at the fancy hotel on the beach around 4 PM. The female bartenders at the beach hotel were young and very pretty. Every time we would down a shot of tequila, they would urge us to have yet another one right after. I stupidly listened to them, while Larry did not. Three hours and eleven or twelve shots later, I was completely drunk. Larry had only had about five or six shots of tequila, and he was tipsy but not completely inebriated like I was. It was right about that time that we realized that our wives were supposed to meet us at the hotel bar at 6 PM. It was now 7 PM. Even in my drunken state I became very worried. Another half hour passed, and our wives finally walked into the hotel bar.

We breathed a long sigh of relief.

Diana and Abby had, depending on how you looked at it, either a harrowing or funny story to tell. They had summoned a taxi around an hour and a half earlier to take them to the beach hotel, but the Mexican taxi driver kept circling the hotel and didn't stop to drop them off. Finally he pulled over on a dirt road and immediately went to the trunk of the car. There he brought out some tequila, some wine, and an assortment of other alcoholic beverages that our wives had never even seen or heard of.

"Let's all have a drink to celebrate two such lovely ladies arriving in the beautiful island paradise of Cancun," said the taxi driver.

"We don't drink," said Abby.

"And you shouldn't be drinking when you're driving us in your taxi," chided my wife.

"Ah, c'mon. We do this all the time in Mehico. I have wine and tequila. What's your choice?"

"We're not drinking with you," said Diana.

"What's the harm in one little drink?"

"Please take us to the hotel to meet our husbands," pleaded Abby.

"My husband is waiting for us, and he's going to be very mad that we're late," stated my wife with determination. "He's a professional boxer, and you don't want to see him when he's angry."

"Ah, you're not much fun anyway," said the resigned taxi driver, and he got back into the taxi.

Now that our wives were safely with us in the hotel bar, I could finally relax. Of course this state of relaxation caused me to have another couple of shots of tequila. Even Diana, who almost never drinks, had her favorite alcoholic beverage, Kahlua and cream. Then she had another.

By the time we finished drinking, it was dark outside and the four of us decided to take a stroll around the hotel grounds. The grounds were huge and very elegant. Eventually we found our way to the pool. Since it was dark there were only a few people scattered around the pool and one or two splashing in the pool.

"I'd love to take a dip in that pool," I said.

"Too bad we didn't bring bathing suits along," said Abby.

"I don't need a bathing suit," I replied and immediately took off my shirt and shorts and jumped in the pool wearing just my undershorts.

I was more than a bit surprised by my impetuousness, but I was really feeling no pain. However, what came next really floored me. My wife took off her blouse and bra and jumped into the pool topless! She was floating around in the pool wearing just her shorts. Jumping into a pool topless would ordinarily be a bit startling for most women, but what made this so unusual was that it was completely out of character for Diana. Diana was extremely conservative in what she said and how she acted.

I was still getting over the fact she had just had a couple of drinks, which was, in itself, extremely unusual, when this impossible turn of events occurred. The same Diana who chastised me for telling dirty jokes, who got embarrassed watching a sex scene in a movie, who would never swear no matter how upset she was, had just taken off her blouse and bra and jumped topless into a pool in front of other people. I kept thinking, "Who is the alien impersonating Diana, and what has she done with my wife?"

After the shock wore off, Diana and I splashed around in the pool for a few minutes and then climbed out of the pool. We found some towels and dried ourselves off. We then went to where our clothes were lying on one of the beach chairs and put them back on. I noticed that my shorts felt lighter and checked to make sure that the items I had in my pockets were still there—my keys and my wallet. My keys were there, but my wallet was missing. All my money and credit cards were gone.

We stumbled around the hotel and somehow eventually found our way to the taxi stand outside. This time the taxi driver did not stop and go to his trunk for liquor; he dropped us off at our hotel, which looked really shabby compared to the beautiful hotel where we had just had such a surreal experience. I climbed into bed and immediately started hallucinating. After I finally fell off into a restless sleep, Diana woke me up the next morning.

"Larry and Abby are here," said Diana. "We told them we'd all go to the beach together today."

"I have a terrible headache, and every time I stand up, I fall back down again," I replied. "Plus I'm a bit confused. I have no idea what day it is today or why I'm in bed. Please tell them we'll catch up with them for dinner tonight."

"Okay. I'll let them know."

By the time dinnertime rolled around, I was not feeling any better. I had drifted off to sleep and started hallucinating again. When Larry and Abby showed up, I had to explain to them that I still couldn't get out of bed but that I was sure that with a good night's sleep we would see them for breakfast the next morning.

But when the next morning rolled around, that was not to be. I had not had a good night's sleep, yet again. In fact I had spent the night again hallucinating, and I still couldn't stand up without getting dizzy. I was also still very confused.

"We'll see you guys for dinner tonight. I'm sure I'll be okay by then."

But when dinnertime rolled around, my situation still hadn't improved, and we again had to cancel plans with Larry and Abby.

"If things don't get better by tomorrow, I'm taking you to the hospital," said Diana.

I couldn't argue with her. Something was wrong with me, and I was starting to believe it was serious.

The next day, which was only two days before we were scheduled to go home, Diana, Larry, and Abby helped me get up, helped me get dressed, and gently guided me into a waiting taxi. When we arrived at the hospital the woman at the check-in desk took one look at me and immediately had the nurses put me in a wheelchair and wheel me in to see the doctor.

"Are you having a good time in Cancun?" asked the doctor.

"Well, I was until three days ago."

"What seems to be the problem?"

"For the last three days I've been hallucinating and throwing up every day. I've also been confused and disoriented, and I barely have enough energy to get out of bed."

"Did you, by any chance, drink some of our marvelous tequila?"

"I had a few drinks."

"How many?"

"About twelve."

"I think you know why you're sick, young man. It was the alcohol. You have alcohol poisoning. When you drink alcohol, the liver has to filter out the alcohol, a toxin, from the blood. However, the liver can process only about one alcoholic drink per hour. Over what period of time did you drink these twelve shots of tequila?"

"Probably over about three hours."

"Well, in three hours your liver was able to filter out only about three of the shots of tequila. That means you had about nine shots of tequila floating around your bloodstream."

"Is that bad?"

"Very bad. You are a lucky young man. Did you know that in Mehico we average ten alcohol poisoning deaths every day?"

"What should I do now?"

"The worst seems to have passed. Just keep drinking water, and your symptoms should subside."

"But I have to fly home in two days. Will I be able to?"

"Let's hope so," was the only thing the Mexican doctor could say, leaving me very nervous.

When the day to return to the States arrived, I was feeling extremely anxious, but I pulled myself out of bed, and with Diana's help I made it to the airport. I was still feeling sick to my stomach and disoriented, but I finally made it back to home sweet home. Although I often look back at this Cancun vacation with fond memories, I have not drunk one ounce of tequila since then!

Chapter 14

THE FAVORITE

On March 30, 1975, Diana gave birth to our second child, Staci. Staci was not born in the same hospital as a famous basketball player, and she did not look like Mel Torme, but her birth signified another milestone for our family and another challenge for me. We now had one boy and one girl. I thought I knew a little bit about raising boys, but I knew absolutely nothing about girls. Raising Staci, especially in her teenage years, was going to be quite a challenge.

Earlier I stated, "All parents have a favorite child. Of course they say they don't, but they do." That was said in the context of my brother and me, and it was something I believed when Robert and I were both kids. I absolutely believed it until I had children. I'm now convinced that children usually believe that their parents have a favorite child; however, when these children become parents and have children of their own, they develop a completely different perspective.

The standing joke in our family is that Staci is the favorite. I'm not sure if Howard and Staci really believe it deep down inside, but it's absolutely not true. However, to this day, that perception still exists. After all, both of my kids reasoned, I use Staci's birthday (0330 for March 30) as the code for the security alarm in my house, as the code for my garage door, and as the code for many other things. But what was I supposed to do? I couldn't use Howard's birthday for my codes. The four digits to express November 11 are 1111. I couldn't use 1111 as my code unless I wanted my house, my garage, and all other items protected by this code to be ransacked by burglars.

As Howard has pointed out to me many times, it's also true that Staci's hospital birth certificate actually contains her correct birthday, March 30, 1975, while Howard's birth certificate does not contain his correct birth date. Howard's birth certificate, from Washington Hospital Center, actually states that Howard was born on October 11, 1969, rather than November 11, 1969.

This discrepancy did not come to light until Howard applied for his passport. He needed to show his birth certificate to prove his citizenship, so he asked us for it. When we gave it to him, we noticed that it had his birthdate as *October* 11, rather than *November* 11. We contacted the hospital and asked the clerk to check hospital records and issue us a new birth certificate with Howard's correct birthdate. We waited and waited but never heard back from the hospital. In the meantime, Howard's planned cruise, for which he needed his passport, was getting closer and closer. Finally we heard from the hospital, but the news was not good. Its records from that time period had been destroyed in a fire, so there was no way to prove Howard's true birth date.

My son was apoplectic. He needed a passport but couldn't get one, since the only document that proved his citizenship listed his birth date as October 11, 1969. He contacted a lawyer who specialized in helping people obtain passports. His lawyer made dozens of phone calls and also visited the Washington, D.C. Passport Agency, all to no avail.

"Do you want the good news or the bad news first?" asked Howard's lawyer.

"Give me the good news first," Howard replied.

"Well, I know how to get your passport," replied the lawyer.

"Wow! That's great news. What's the bad news?"

"To get your passport, all you have to do is list October 11, 1969, as your date of birth."

"But that's not my date of birth."

"I know."

"My license and all my other documents list my date of birth as the correct date, November 11, 1969."

"I know."

"I feel funny lying about my date of birth on my passport."

"I know."

"Well, I guess if that's the only way to get a passport, I have no choice, but I really don't feel good about this."

"I know."

To this day Howard's passport lists his date of birth as October 11, while his driver's license and other documents list his date of birth as November 11. He lives in fear that, one day, someone in Customs will ask to see both documents and refuse to let him back into the country.

And, of course, he blames us.

"How come you messed up my birth certificate and not Staci's?" Howard has asked us many times.

"We didn't do it on purpose," I reply.

Howard is aware that this was just one of those crazy things that happens, but he still brings it up every time the "favorite" discussion arises as further proof that Staci is the favorite.

One area, however, in which Diana and I certainly did not favor Staci was in the rules we set for both of our children, especially when they were teenagers. Howard, being the first born, got to experience these rules first.

We had rules against drinking before our kids were of the legal age to drink, strict rules against driving and drinking (in case they ignored the previous rule), rules about where our kids could go after dark, and rules about curfews. We had rules about the types of parties they could go to and who they could have in the car with them right after they got their driver's license. In Maryland, during the first year after obtaining a driver's license, drivers under the age of 18 could not drive past midnight and could not drive with others in the car, except for immediate family members.

Howard often flouted many of these rules. And we let him.

We were angry when he got home after midnight, ignoring the restriction on his driver's license against driving after midnight. We yelled at him for doing it, but he kept doing it over and over. We occasionally grounded him for this infraction, but when we allowed him to drive again, he would continue to violate this restriction. He violated our curfew and frequented parties we told him he could not attend. Although it exasperated and frustrated us, we allowed it to continue. Deep down we knew he had a good set of friends, and as a boy, we were pretty sure Howard could take care of himself.

When Staci became a teenager, she was faced with the same rules and tried to break them even more often than Howard had. Staci was naturally more adventuresome and more rebellious than Howard was then and continues to be so to this day. She obtained a fake ID that enabled her to drink illegally, and she attempted to go to bars that would serve her alcohol. She tried to attend parties that we told her she could not attend. And when she was not yet 18 years old, she, like her brother had done five years before, wanted to drive after midnight. We wouldn't let her do any of those things. As opposed to turning a blind eye to many of Howard's youthful indiscretions, we were overly strict when Staci attempted to do many of the same things.

"Why did Howard get to drive after midnight when he had a probationary license?" asked Staci. "And why did you allow Howard to use his fake ID to buy booze, yet you confiscated my fake ID? Furthermore, how come you let Howard go to whatever parties he wanted but won't let me go to hardly any parties?"

"It's very simple, Stace," I responded. "It's called the double standard."

Staci looked at me with the look she reserved for incredibly stupid comments. "That's sexist, you know," responded my daughter.

"No, it's sexist to *treat* men and women differently, but it's *not* sexist to *raise* boys and girls differently. Teenage boys and teenage girls are completely different, and different rules need to be applied to boys versus girls."

Although that answer clearly didn't satisfy my daughter, it's something I believe with all my heart.

Not only did we raise Howard and Staci differently, but also both Diana and I did different activities with Staci than we did with Howard. I played ball with Howard and coached all of his basketball and baseball teams, while Diana went shopping and did other activities with Staci.

The conversations we had with each of our children were completely different. I talked about sports with Howard and had almost no conversations about social problems he may have encountered in getting through his teenage years. Conversely, Diana's and my conversations with Staci were about almost nothing else other than Staci's teenage social problems. Almost every day during Staci's teenage years resulted in another traumatic event in her life, and they all revolved around boys and dating.

Boys Staci liked didn't call her. She wasn't invited to parties that she felt she should have been. She broke up with her boyfriend and cried herself to sleep. And this was all in just one week!

While Howard's teenage years went by very quickly, Staci's teenage years seemed to drag on forever. There were a few anxious moments with Howard. On two occasions we had to rush him to the hospital after he broke some bones while playing ball and he had a few issues with one of the girls on our street, but all in all, his teenage years were devoid of drama.

But drama was Staci's middle name. Literally every day or two resulted in some traumatic event in Staci's life.

When Staci was approaching her sixteenth birthday, we decided to give her a Sweet Sixteen party.

"Invite a few of your friends," Diana and I told Staci.

"How many can I invite?"

"A few."

"But I can't choose among them."

When all was said and done, Staci's Sweet Sixteen party consisted of Staci and 150 of her closest friends.

Staci went to the University of Maryland, as did her brother. Because she went to a state university and, thus, saved us a lot of money, we agreed to let her spend a semester abroad. She chose Australia, about as far away from home as she could get. She loved Australia and, of course, met a boy there whom she began dating. If Staci's social issues in the U.S. created endless drama, having a boyfriend in Australia, whom she had to leave to come back to the States, reached new heights in drama.

Staci arrived back from Australia about a week before Howard was about to get married.

"I'm not going to Howard's wedding without Dylan," Staci proclaimed.

"But your boyfriend is five thousand miles away," Diana and I explained to our daughter.

"I don't care! I'm not going without him."

After staying up all night and crying for her first five days after returning from Australia, Staci eventually calmed down. She was 19 years old then, and we were thankful that she would be a teenage girl for only one more year.

We learned that teenage boys and teenage girls were unbelievably different, and each had their own sets of strengths and weaknesses. We learned a lot about parenthood and really enjoyed every minute of raising our kids. And we raised them without playing favorites!

Chapter 15

LITTLE SQUIRREL, BIG NUT

$\mathcal{J}$ was a big sports fan, but Howard became an even bigger sports fan. He watched and played sports incessantly. He became a Mets fan in baseball and a Giants fan in football, even though I never urged him to root for the same teams for which I rooted. After all, Howard grew up in the Maryland suburbs. Football and baseball teams in Washington, D.C., and to some extent Baltimore were the natural teams to root for. They were the teams all of his friends rooted for. D.C was only a twenty-minute drive away from our home and Baltimore was about forty minutes away. But he rooted for the teams I rooted for, not for his neighborhood teams.

I believe that this phenomenon is part of what I had observed about raising kids in general. Kids rarely listen to their parents, but they mimic all their actions. I've observed parents who smoke or drink alcohol excessively telling their kids not to drink or smoke. The kids invariably end up smoking or drinking because they observed their parents doing exactly that. I'm sure that's what happened with Howard's rooting interests in sports. He watched me fervently rooting for the Mets and Giants, so he did the same, without having to be told.

From the age of seven years old, Howard started playing all sports. I coached him almost every year in basketball and baseball.

One day, when Howard was about 14 years old, he said to me, "Dad, I think I want to play soccer this year."

"Okay, when and where is it?" I replied.

"Every Wednesday at the soccer field by my school."

"Not a problem. I'll drive you to your games."

"But I want you to coach me."

I had coached Howard's basketball and baseball teams without fail every year, but coaching soccer was a completely different matter. I loathed soccer. It was too boring for me. Watching a game for two hours and watching the teams score just one or perhaps two goals in the whole game was not for me. Additionally I knew nothing about the rules of soccer or the strategy.

"I can't coach soccer, Howard," I replied.

"Why not?"

"Because I know nothing about the game. I don't even understand the rules."

"But you can learn," pleaded my son.

Reluctantly and with much trepidation, I agreed to coach Howard's soccer team.

Shortly after I was notified that my request to coach soccer had been approved by the local recreation league (yay), I received the roster of boys who would be on the team. I scheduled the first practice for the following day.

"Okay, guys, kick the soccer ball around," I told the boys on my team.

The boys kicked the soccer ball around for about fifteen minutes.

"What do we do next?" asked one of the boys.

I was completely stumped, but I noticed another coach, only about thirty yards away, conducting practice for his team, so I walked to where they were practicing. The coach had a foreign accent and I overheard him telling his team that he was from Brazil.

My ears perked up. I knew that soccer was incredibly popular in Brazil and the fans were fervid and very knowledgeable. Brazilians really knew their soccer. I got as close as I could to him, without being conspicuous, and listened to what he said.

"Don't bunch up," he kept imploring his team.

That made sense to me. If teammates were too close to each other, passing to other teammates would be difficult, and the opposing team could defend them easily. I went back to my team.

"Mr. Skall, where did you go?" asked one boy.

"I went to scout one of the opposing teams," I replied.

"So what do we do now?" asked the same boy. "What's our strategy?"

"Don't bunch up," I replied.

"Okay. What else?"

"That's all you really need to know. Just don't bunch up, pass the ball around, and score goals."

I knew soccer strategy should have been much more comprehensive than this, but that was all I had.

Our team played ten games in the league. In our first nine games, we were shut out. We finally scored a goal in our tenth and last game, but we lost that game as well.

We ended the season 0-10. Not bunching up was sound strategy but clearly there had to be more to soccer strategy than that.

At the end of the summer, right after the soccer debacle ended, Staci approached me with a request. "Dad, you always coach Howard's teams, but you've never coached any of my teams," she said. "You even coached Howard's soccer team, and you hate soccer."

Staci had a good point. Staci had been on one or two softball and basketball teams, and Diana and I had gone to all of her games, but I had never coached any of her teams. Even though she was only nine years old at the time and had been playing sports for only a couple of years, she was absolutely correct. The double standard should not apply here.

A new girls' basketball league was forming in the fall, so I signed up to coach Staci's basketball team. I was excited about the opportunity. I was feeling guilty about never coaching any of Staci's teams, and basketball was my favorite sport to play and coach, so I was really looking forward to it.

I conducted a few practices, taught the girls how to shoot and how to play defense, and the team and I were ready to play our first game.

The game was a close and exciting game, but in the third quarter, one of the players on my team, with a few others, ran for a loose ball and came out of the scrum crying. Fearing a broken bone or some other serious injury, I immediately ran onto the court.

"What happened, Marcy?" I asked. "Where did you hurt yourself?"

"I didn't hurt myself," Marcy replied.

"Why were you crying then?"

"I broke one of my nails," Marcy said and burst out in tears again.

The other girls hugged Marcy, and they all walked off the court together.

"Okay, girls," I said. "Let's regroup."

"What does that mean?" asked another one of the girls.

"It means let's forget what happened and focus on playing the rest of the game."

"But how can we play the rest of the game if Marcy broke her nail?" a different girl asked.

"We can't play anymore, Dad," Staci explained. "Marcy broke her nail."

My first experience in coaching girls' basketball ended with the team in distress and a loss on the scoreboard because of a for-feit. Coaching young girls was quite a bit different from coaching young boys.

Although coaching Staci in sports didn't turn out to be a rous-ing success, we still did a lot of other things together. I'm not an outdoorsman, to say the least, and as a boy and then as an adult I never wanted to go camping. Camping implied sleeping out-side in tents, on hard ground, with insects and other animals all around. Furthermore, in the winter you had to provide your own heat by making fires, and worse, in the summer, there was no air-conditioning. Why anyone would want to torture themselves like this was beyond me. I used to joke that Jews don't like camping or any other form of roughing it. Roughing it for Jews, I liked to say, was staying at the Holiday Inn.

For those reasons when I was a kid, I never considered join-ing the Boy Scouts or Cub Scouts, and neither did Howard. However, around the time Staci was 12 or 13, a new organization that I had never heard of started becoming popular. It was called Indian Guides (for boys) and Indian Princesses (for girls).

The Indian Guides/Princesses was founded in 1926 by Harold Keltner, director of the YMCA St. Louis chapter. The Indian Guides Program was inspired by an Obijway Indian named Joe Friday. In fact, Jack Webb, an Indian Guides alumnus, got his character inspiration for his role in the hugely popular TV show *Dragnet*, from this real Joe Friday.

Friday guided Keltner on fishing and hunting trips, and ac-cording to Y literature, he once described to Keltner his people's philosophy for father-son relationships. "The Indian father raises his son," Friday is quoted as saying. "He teaches his son to hunt, track, fish, walk softly and silently in the forest, know the mean-ing and purpose of life and all he must know, while the white man allows another to raise his son."

The Indian Guides program was developed to help foster stronger father/son bonds. The program was later expanded to include Indian Princesses, which fostered stronger father/daughter bonds.

Wearing headbands, feathers, and beads the "tribe" of fathers and sons/daughters would meet regularly at one of the parents' homes to perform typical Indian rituals. But the highlights of Indian Guides/Princesses were the weekend campouts held several times a year in designated campgrounds, such as state parks. The purpose of these campouts was to simulate the American Indians' strong tradition of being independent outdoorsmen who could live independently in the forest.

Indian Princesses sounded like a way to have fun and learn a thing or two about camping. As an added bonus, I figured, we would acquire expertise in some of the same activities that the Boy Scouts taught, like how to set up a camp, make a fire to stay warm, and navigate successfully through the woods. Staci and I were really excited to join, but the first thing we needed to do was to come up with Indian names for both of us.

"I think I like the name Little Squirrel," said Staci.

"Perfect," I replied. "Then I can be Big Nut."

"That fits you to a T," Staci replied, while laughing hysterically. I was hoping she was laughing with me, rather than at me, but I didn't think so.

As Little Squirrel and Big Nut we eagerly awaited our first camping experience. The first campout was held at Camp Letts in Edgewater, Maryland, in November of 1987. Although I was a bit squeamish about sleeping in tents and making fires to keep us warm, I was really stoked about sharing this bond with my daughter. Howard and I bonded over sports and now Staci and I had the opportunity to create just as strong a bond. But who would have thought our bond would be over camping?

We arrived at Camp Letts and settled in. To my relief I found out that we did not have to sleep on the ground in tents. Staci and I were given bunk beds in an old bungalow. Next came the challenge of making dinner for the tribe. I had heard from previous Indian Princess fathers that most tribes brought hot dogs and hamburgers to grill. But not our tribe. Luckily, we ended up in a tribe with fathers who were gourmet cooks, and those fathers insisted on being the ones to cook. While other tribes were munching on hot dogs and baked beans, we were eating an appetizer of clams casino, with filet mignon as our entrée, and I wasn't doing any of the cooking. I could really get used to this camping thing.

After dinner, while the girls were chatting away happily, the fathers played poker and drank beer, lots of beer. The next morning I woke up a bit hung over to the whirring sound of chain saws. I had never used a chain saw in my life. The rest of the men were cutting down trees to make firewood to keep us warm. I laid in my bunk hoping they knew what they were doing and a tree wouldn't fall on Staci or me.

But all went well. During the three days at Camp Letts, we stayed warm over a campfire with the wood the other men had salvaged from the trees. We ate to our hearts content with the food the other men prepared, and I won lots of money from these same men, playing poker. I did provide the beer, though. Finally, something I could do!

All in all, Indian Princesses proved to be a blast. Staci and I bonded and got much closer. Little Squirrel made lots of new friends, and Big Nut learned that our Native American friends apparently appreciated great food, good beer, and fun-filled poker games.

Chapter 16

DOES ANYBODY HAVE A MICROPHONE?

By the time Staci and I bonded at Camp Letts in November of 1987, I had been working for a different government agency for almost nine years. DTMB was a good place to work, but I was becoming complacent and stagnant there. In fact I was flat out bored with my job, so I started to look for new jobs.

Right down the road from where I lived and worked there was a place called the National Bureau of Standards (NBS) that was nationally known. It did research and produced standards in many areas, including physics, chemistry, and building and fire research, among others. More importantly to me, they performed cutting-edge research in computer science and had just decided to expand its work in this area. NBS was the cream of the crop of federal agencies. Well over half of its employees had PhDs, and the agency and the people working for it were very well respected.

NBS was founded in 1901, heeding the call from the nation's scientists and industrialists to establish an authoritative domestic measurement and standards laboratory.

The need for standards was never more apparent than during the great Baltimore fire of 1904. This fire raged in Baltimore on Sunday, February 7, and Monday, February 8, 1904. More than 1,230 firefighters tried to keep the blaze under control. The fire quickly outstripped the ability of the city's firefighters to fight the blaze. Engine companies from Washington, D.C., transported by train, arrived in Baltimore to assist in firefighting a few hours after the fire started. Other fire companies from surrounding areas, such as Altoona, Harrisburg, Wilmington, Atlantic City, New York, and Philadelphia also arrived to join the effort. However, to everyone's dismay, the hoses from the various jurisdictions would not fit the Baltimore hydrants, because of the difference in the threads, thus not allowing any of the firefighters from neighboring areas to help. The fire, consequently, burned until 5 PM the next afternoon and was not brought under control for thirty hours, resulting in massive devastation.

A study by NBS revealed that there were six hundred sizes and variations in fire-hose couplings across the country. Fortunately, the events that occurred at the great Baltimore fire led to the adoption of a national standard for fire hydrant connection nozzles, led by NBS. These specifications remain today as the current standard for fire hydrants. NBS truly did work that was extremely important, and it was somewhere I would love to work.

Thinking that I had no chance of getting a job at this prestigious agency that had such a long and colorful history, I offhandedly submitted my résumé, but to my surprise I was accepted for the job! I started work there in October 1978.

I ended up working at NBS (which subsequently changed its name to the National Institute of Standards and Technology, or NIST) until my "retirement" in 2009. After my official retirement in 2009 I continued to do contract work for NIST and other federal agencies and still do, to this day.

Earlier in the same year that Staci and I experienced our first campout at Camp Letts in November 1987, I found myself on a business trip for NIST. At that time I was the manager of the Graphics Software Group at NIST, and on Saturday, January

20, 1987, I arrived in Denver, Colorado, to attend a computer graphics standards meeting with graphics experts from around the world. The meeting started on Monday, January 22.

Ordinarily I would arrive on Sunday to attend a Monday meeting, but this particular Sunday was no ordinary Sunday. It was the Sunday when my beloved New York Football Giants were scheduled to play the Denver Broncos in the Super Bowl at the Rose Bowl in Pasadena, California. In fact, the Giants had never before been to the Super Bowl. It was the very first Super Bowl in Giants history, and I was certainly not going to miss it by being on an airplane.

I therefore arrived in Denver on Saturday with a colleague of mine, Susie Quinn. Susie was a deeply religious Catholic and always attended Mass on Sunday. On Sunday morning she asked me to drive her to Mass in a different area of Denver from where we were staying. Knowing that we would be back in plenty of time for the big game, I agreed.

When we arrived at the church (which I later found out was the largest Catholic church in downtown Denver) there was a large line forming to get into the church. Susie and I got in line and were two of the last people to make it into Mass before the church had to start turning people away, because of the enormous size of the crowd on that Super Bowl Sunday.

I had never been to a Catholic Mass, and I really had no idea what to expect. The priest started the Mass by saying he was sorry that the church had to turn people away because this Sunday was such a special day, the day the city's revered Denver Broncos were going to crush the New York Giants. The pun got my attention since the Broncos were nicknamed the Orange Crush. The people at the mass all stood up and applauded.

I was feeling weird and a bit guilty that all the other people could not get into this historic Mass. If they only knew that not only was I not Catholic, but I also was a rabid Giants fan, they probably would have thrown me out on my ear.

However, it all worked out perfectly for me, as the Giants won their first Super Bowl ever by defeating the Denver Broncos 39-20. The victory ended a long drought. This Super Bowl win on January 21, 1987 was the Giants first NFL title since 1956, when they defeated the Chicago Bears 47-7.

The year 1987 was a really good year for me. Bonding with Staci at Indian Princesses (including the fun card game and delicious clams casino), and the fact that the Giants had won the Super Bowl put me in a celebratory mood, so when Diana started discussing New Year's Eve right after I returned from Camp Letts with Staci in November of 1987, I was more receptive than usual.

New Year's was never a big deal to me, but for some reason it was always a really big deal to Diana. Diana had to go out every New Year's Eve. Sometimes we went to dinner with friends and then went back to one of our houses afterwards to watch the ball drop. At other times we went to a small party with friends and watched the ball drop. Occasionally, we went to a big bash with a small group of friends that we knew and a larger group of people who were strangers and, of course, watched the ball drop. But we had never strayed far from home to celebrate New Year's Eve.

That all changed on December 31, 1987. Diana and I were looking for something new and exciting to do to welcome in the New Year, and I wanted to celebrate 1987 with as much gusto as I could.

We mentioned New Year's Eve to our friends Billy and Janet, and they were interested in celebrating with us. We all got together to discuss where we would go. We did some research and found out that the beach town of Ocean City, Maryland, was having a big New Year's Eve gala at one of its fanciest hotels. Ordinarily, Ocean City was packed with tourists in the summer but was a ghost town in the winter. We had gone there in the summer with the kids and found it to be very crowded with lots of traffic. Also, there were screaming kids everywhere we turned. Spending time in Ocean City without traffic and screaming kids sounded very appealing to us.

We all decided to celebrate New Year's Eve at a party in the Carousel Hotel in Ocean City. Howard was way too old to celebrate New Year's Eve with his parents, but Staci was not, at least in our opinion. Thus, we packed up the car and Diana, Staci, and I drove three hours to Ocean City, Maryland. We met Billy, Janet, and their son, Lee, there. Lee was 12 years old, the same age as Staci.

New Year's Eve was Thursday evening, so we arrived at the hotel on Tuesday and planned to stay for three nights. We had nice quiet dinners on both Tuesday and Wednesday nights. Lee and Staci enjoyed each other's company, and the two days were uneventful.

Then came Thursday night—New Year's Eve. The adults were all dressed up and the kids, reluctantly, followed suit. The hotel's New Year's Eve package included a fancy steak-and-lobster dinner, but more importantly also included an open bar.

Wanting to get our money's worth at the open bar, we all arrived at the New Year's gala at 7 PM, the earliest we were allowed in. Janet and I started drinking from the time we walked through the door. Our respective spouses were looking at each other and shaking their heads because both Janet and I were known to like to drink quite a bit at these types of occasions.

I was a very moderate drinker, probably having only two or three drinks a week at most. However, when I did drink, as in many other things in my life, I tended to do it to excess. I was, of course, very careful never to drink and drive, but I figured that having a good time by drinking a bit too much was not going to hurt me (with the exception of the fiasco in Cancun).

I've seen mean drunks, angry drunks, and drunks who sat in a corner and sulked. But I was a happy drunk. The more I drank, the happier I got, and I was never angry, sad, or abrasive. From my experience hanging out with Janet, she was much the same way.

Thus, Janet and I drank, and then we drank some more, and we were both in a particularly good and very happy mood. At about 10 PM, the band started playing and, as 12 o'clock approached, Janet and I decided we wanted to sing along with the band. We went up on stage with the band and then we decided to walk from table to table, serenading the guests. On stage we had a microphone, but the band wouldn't let us take it with us. Thus when we walked from table to table while singing, we decided that we needed a different microphone, or at least a microphone prop.

At first we used the glasses that we had emptied of vodka to sing into, but that just didn't feel right. Glasses didn't look or feel like microphones, but an empty bottle would. We searched high and low for some empty Coke bottles, but alas, none were available.

Janet had an idea. "Wait," she said. "I have the perfect thing to use as a microphone." Janet reached into her purse and removed two tampons! With tampons in hand, Janet and I continued to walk around from table to table, serenading some very shocked strangers.

As Janet and I ambled back to our table after our performance, we noticed that our children, Staci and Lee, had hidden under the table, so as not to be associated in any way with us.

As with every other year, Diana and I were planning to watch the ball drop at midnight, but unlike all the other years, I have absolutely no recollection of that event, because I had passed out!

Chapter 17

ESPN THE APHRODISIAC

J wanted 1988 to start with a bang, but since I was passed out at midnight, it seemed more like a whimper. Despite not being awake to see the ball drop, I had a lots of fun on New Year's Eve with Billy and Janet, but sadly, it was back to work for Diana and me shortly thereafter. We both liked our jobs, so work wasn't too much of a strain, but as summer got closer and closer, we began talking about taking a summer vacation. Although we had taken a few vacations at the beach, we still hadn't done what I had always wanted to do: go on a cruise.

I had wanted to go on a cruise for a long time. I had even suggested a cruise for our honeymoon, but in 1967 cruises weren't as popular as they became later. In fact Norwegian Cruise Lines had just been founded the year before, in 1966. Royal Caribbean (founded in 1968) and Carnival Cruise Lines (founded in 1972) were not yet in existence. My suggestion to go on a romantic cruise for our honeymoon fell on completely deaf ears. Diana refused even to consider going on a cruise for our honeymoon.

I guess that's why it was such a shock to me when all of a sudden, in the summer of 1988, Diana suggested that we go on a cruise.

"You know, we've never been on a cruise," said Diana.

"Well, that's because you hate cruises," I said.

"Why do you say that?"

"Because you laughed at me when I suggested we go on a cruise for our honeymoon."

"That was different. No one goes on a cruise for their honeymoon."

"Actually, they do."

"Well, it doesn't matter. I would really like to go on a cruise now. Bob and Carol go with Mitch and Sandy all the time."

Bob and Carol were two of our oldest friends. In fact, I am almost related to Carol. My father's brother, Frank, was married to Carol's mother's sister, Ann. Even though we're not related, I've known Carol almost my entire life. Ever since I was about 12 years old, I remember going to Uncle Frank and Aunt Ann's house and seeing Carol there. I noticed her at these gatherings because Carol was incredibly attractive. We weren't close then, and she was a girl, so I never spoke to her, and I felt like we had nothing in common. However, in Carol's mind we are related, and Diana and I became very close to her and her husband, Bob, as soon as they moved from New York City to Maryland in the early 1970s.

Mitch and Sandy were Bob and Carol's best friends and were good friends of ours, as well. In fact, Bob and Carol and Mitch and Sandy all shared season tickets with us to the Washington Capitals hockey team, starting when the team was founded in 1974.

Up until 1974 I had never rooted for a professional Washington sports team. As a fanatic New York Giants fan, I naturally hated the Washington Redskins. I actually received almost as much enjoyment out of seeing the Redskins lose as I did in seeing the Giants win. Also I still rooted fanatically for the New York Mets, so I had absolutely no interest in following the poorly performing Washington Senators franchise.

However, my rooting interest in the New York Rangers, which was always fairly minimal to begin with, was pretty much non-existent by the time the NHL added two expansion franchises in 1974—the Washington Capitals and the Kansas City Scouts. It was time to have a local professional sports team to root for, and Bob, Mitch, and I became huge Washington Capitals fans.

Rooting for a Washington hockey team, however, did nothing to diminish my passion for the New York Giants and the New York Mets. In fact when Diana approached me about going on a cruise in the summer of 1988, the Mets were in first place in the NL East, on their way to winning the National East Championship with a 100-60 record.

I, of course, could not go on a cruise unless I knew that I could watch the Mets games on the ship or, at the very least, could find out the Mets score and watch highlights of the games on ESPN.

ESPN was founded in 1979 by Bill Rasmussen and his son, Scott, as America's first twenty-four-hour sports network. In 1979, there were no twenty-four-hour networks, not even NBC, ABC, or CBS. HBO didn't exist then and neither did MTV, CNN, or Fox. ESPN forever changed the way we watched sports once it was unleashed upon sports fans on September 7, 1979.

By1988 ESPN was well established and had become as central to my existence as food and water. Thus when Diana and I started making plans with Bob and Carol and Mitch and Sandy, I made it a point to ask them whether or not the ship we were going on provided access to ESPN. Mitch and Sandy were the cruise veterans, having been on at least five or six prior cruises, and they assured me that watching ESPN would not be a problem.

Diana and I were excited to go on our first cruise. The cruise was on the Royal Caribbean, and we were cruising to various islands in the Caribbean, including Jamaica, Barbados, Antigua, and the Bahamas.

The six of us flew to Miami and stayed there overnight. The next day we boarded the ship. Once we had gotten through the interminable waiting lines to review our documents, we finally were able to see our rooms, which, I learned, cruise ships call cabins. Our cabin was nice but ridiculously small and a bit claustrophobic. I don't believe cabins with balconies were available in 1988, but if they were, we didn't have such a cabin. We did have a port hole so we could, at least, look out at the ocean.

However, we couldn't see too much of the ocean through a tiny round window that was, at most, two feet in diameter. I made it a point to frequent the main deck to watch the ocean. There, unrestricted by having to peer through a tiny piece of glass, the view of the ocean was magnificent. I have always loved the ocean. Whenever I would go on a work trip to a city on the ocean like Los Angeles or San Diego, the very first thing I would do, right after I checked into the hotel, was to drive to the ocean. I would then find a bench, sit down, and stare at the ocean.

The vastness of the ocean had a peaceful and calming influence on me. No matter what was bothering me, no matter what work pressure I was under or how nervous I was about an upcoming presentation, just staring at the ocean was the only therapy I would need to relax. Shrinks and yoga and other forms of therapy cost a lot more money, but in my opinion were not nearly as effective at calming one's nerves as staring at the never-ending undulating waves of the ocean.

On the ship I was staring out at the ocean, in my own little world, when I heard a loud, blaring noise from the ship's loudspeakers.

"We will now have our safety drill," someone from the ship told us.

"What's going on?" I asked Sandy.

"It's just routine," replied Sandy. "They show you what to do if the ship is about to capsize."

"About to what?" I replied.

"Don't worry about it," Sandy told me in a reassuring voice. "They just show you where the lifeboats are, how to get into them, and what to do."

"But Diana gets scared in a rowboat," I said. "How would she handle something like that?" I shrewdly made it seem like I was selflessly concerned about my wife rather than me.

"Just relax," said Sandy. "Right after this drill, you can go to your cabin and watch ESPN."

That cheered me up and calmed my nerves.

We eventually got through the safety drill, even though one of the ship's helpers had to twice show me how to put on my life jacket.

Right after the drill ended, the six of us went right back to our cabins. By then all of the luggage had been delivered and our suitcases were waiting for us in our rooms. Diana immediately went to her suitcase and started putting clothes into dresser drawers and hanging other items on hangers.

"There are not enough hangers," Diana lamented. "Plus, there are hardly any drawers. Where are we going to put everything?"

I was not making any attempt to put my clothes away, nor was I listening to anything Diana was saying. Instead I had turned on the TV, and I was frantically going through all the channels.

I saw lots of movie channels with movies that I had absolutely no interest in ever watching. I saw some news channels, and I found a channel on the TV that showed live reports by the captain. I even found a sports channel, but it was showing soccer. Soccer! What I clearly did not find was ESPN.

I was frantic. "Diana," I cried out. "There's no ESPN!"

"What is that? Some kind of channel where people talk to

other people just by using their minds? Or is that when people try to predict the future?"

"No," I said, clearly exasperated. "That's ESP—extrasensory perception. Mental telepathy and clairvoyance are all part of ESP, not ESPN. ESPN is a sports channel, and it's the only way I can watch Met highlights or even see baseball scores at all."

"Well, who told you the ship could get ESPN?" my wife asked me calmly.

"Sandy. Sandy told me we would get ESPN on the ship. She guaranteed it."

"Well, go speak to her."

I left my cabin. "Sandy," I called out. "Sandy, where are you?"

The door opened from a cabin a few doors down, and Sandy popped her head out.

"Sandy, there's no ESPN."

"Let me check," said Sandy.

"I just checked a hundred times. There's no ESPN!"

"Okay. Just let me unpack, and we'll try to figure this out."

"You can unpack later," I said as I pulled Sandy out of her cabin. "What are we going to do?" I asked her dejectedly.

"I have an idea," said Sandy. "We'll go to the reception desk. They know everything that happens on a ship, and they also know how to get anything done."

Sandy took me to a different deck and led me through a labyrinth of entranceways before we finally arrived at the reception desk.

"Isn't the ship supposed to have ESPN?" asked Sandy.

"I thought so," answered a young man named Edward.

"Well, it doesn't," I cried out.

"Okay. Let me check," said Edward.

After a few minutes of looking thorough various papers, Edward looked at us and said, "It says right here that the satellite dish is capable of getting ESPN."

"Great," I said, while letting out an audible sigh of relief.

"But I still can't seem to tune in ESPN on the satellite dish," Edward said, ending my short-lived minute of happiness.

"I really need ESPN. I'd do anything to have it on the ship."

Then Sandy said something that shocked even me. I'll say almost anything to anybody, and I rarely get shocked by something someone else says, but this rendered me speechless.

"The two of us just got married," Sandy lied. "And we're on our honeymoon. We were really looking forward to a romantic cruise, but to tell you the truth, my husband can't get it up without ESPN."

I couldn't tell if Edward was going to laugh or yell at us, but he did neither. He just looked at us sadly and said, "I just figured out what happened. Even though we are capable of receiving ESPN broadcasts, we need a subscription to ESPN for our guests to be able to view that station. All of our other ships have an ESPN subscription, but since this is the newest and most expensive of all of our ships, we were way over budget and had to cut costs. Although we have the capability to get ESPN, we canceled the service to save money."

"Thanks for nothing," said Sandy. "No sex for us on our honeymoon!"

Chapter 18

MY WIFE THE EXORCIST

*A*lthough our first cruise disappointed me because I could not watch my beloved Mets or even find out the scores of their games, Diana had a great time. And I had to admit, even without ESPN, I had a great time too. The food was fabulous and, perhaps more importantly, it was unlimited. I could certainly get used to two or three portions of filet mignon and lobster for dinner every night. Lounging in the sunshine of the pool was very relaxing, and working out in the gym, while watching the undulating waves of the ocean, was both healthy and relaxing. The shows at night were extremely entertaining, and we met tons of new and interesting people.

After we returned home, I finally admitted to Diana that I really enjoyed the cruise and a few years later, after ESPN became standard on all cruise lines, Diana and I decided to go on another cruise. We went with two other couples with whom we had become very friendly. One of our friends' sisters was a travel agent and got us a particularly good deal on a cruise whose ports of call included many Caribbean islands, specifically Barbados, San Juan, Antigua, St. Thomas, and St. Maarten.

Although this ship offered numerous excursions, our group decided we'd explore the islands on our own. The stops at the first few ports of call were both uneventful and predictable. The girls went shopping in the local towns and the guys either went to the local beaches or just had a few drinks in one of the bars on the main drag. However, by the time the ship stopped in St. Maarten, we decided to get much more adventurous.

I had researched St. Maarten and found out everything there was to know about that island. I found out that St. Maarten is an island in the northeast Caribbean Sea. In 1493 Columbus embarked on his second voyage to the New World. Columbus came across St. Maarten on November 11, 1493, the feast day of Saint Marten of Tours, and may have stopped there. In honor of this saint, Columbus named the island San Martin, which later got translated to St. Maarten (in French) and Sint Maarten (in Dutch).

St. Maarten is about thirty-four square miles in area and is almost equally divided between the French and Dutch parts. A slightly greater part is under the sovereignty of France than the Netherlands, but the two parts are roughly equal in population. The island of St. Maarten is the only land that shares a border between France and the Netherlands. There is no border between these two countries in Europe. Both the French and Dutch parts of St. Maarten have many hills with large mountain peaks.

There are many beautiful beaches in St. Maarten, but in my research the one that caught my eye was Orient Bay Beach, one of the most famous nude beaches in the world. Once I read about it and told everyone else about it, we decided that we had to get to Orient Beach.

There were many ways we could have gotten to Orient Beach. The ship offered an excursion to Orient Beach. Just as easily, we could have disembarked from the ship and taken a taxi to St. Maarten. But, no, we had to get to the nude beach in the most difficult manner possible.

We decided to rent a car from one of the local rental places and drive to St. Maarten. We all had a terrible sense of direction, but that fact didn't deter us from embarking on this great adventure.

As we left the ship, we saw a sign for car rentals, and we randomly went to the first counter.

"We'd like to rent a car for six people," I said.

"No problem," replied the man behind the counter. "We have jeeps that hold six people."

"Great," I replied and handed the man my credit card.

"Whoever will be the driver, please come with me," the man behind the counter said.

"Who wants to drive?" I asked the crew. "I'm guessing the car will be a stick shift, rather than an automatic, so who can drive a stick?"

"Not me," replied my friend Steve.

"Not me either," his wife, Sue, chimed in.

"Not me," replied my friend Jay.

"Certainly, not me," his wife, Doreen, replied.

Knowing Diana had never driven a stick shift either, I realized that I was going to be the driver.

"I'll go with you," I finally said to the man behind the counter.

I walked about twenty-five yards down the road with the man, and he got into a car.

"Please get in," he said.

"Why?" I asked

"Because I need to take you to the jeep."

I got in the car with the man, hoping I would not be kidnapped, and we drove about another two miles down the road until we arrived at a small house. Parked right in front of the house was an old open-air jeep. There was a driver's seat, a passenger's seat, and a bench seat in the back that looked like it could fit three people, but only if the people were very small or packed very closely together.

"Here's the jeep. Isn't she a beauty?" asked the man. "I've kept her in great shape for fifteen years"

"But we have six people. How are we going to fit six people in there?"

"Oh, it's not a problem. Four people can sit in the back. You'll only be in the jeep for a short while, no?"

"I don't know. We want to go to Orient Beach. How far is that?"

"Oh, it's only a ten-minute drive."

Well, in for a penny, in for a pound, I thought, and the man and I both got into the jeep and drove back to where everyone was waiting for us.

When the man from the rental car company and I arrived back at the rental counter, I was greeted with shocked looks from the rest of our party.

"Are you kidding me?" asked Doreen "We all can't fit into that car. My fat ass alone will take up most of the back seat."

"Mark, this is crazy," Sue chimed in.

"Well, it's all we got," I answered. "Do we want to go to Orient Beach or not?"

"Let's do this," said Jay, always the optimist. "It's a beautiful day, and we get to ride in an open-air jeep."

So we all climbed into the jeep. Steve, who had the longest legs, went into the front passenger seat, and the other four, crammed like sardines, reluctantly climbed into the back seat.

Although the GPS was invented in 1957 during the Sputnik era, it was not yet commonplace in cars during the early 1990s, when we were exploring St. Maarten and trying to find Orient Beach. Mazda invented the Mazda Eunos Cosmo Navigation System for cars in 1990, but it was available only in gadget-loving Japan. It was not until 1998, when Garmin introduced its first portable StreetPilot navigation system for automotive use, that a GPS became viable in the U.S. Even though the first smart phone was invented in 1992 and released for purchase in 1994, no one could have confused it with the modern-day smartphone. It was big and bulky and certainly was not capable of providing turn-by-turn navigation instructions.

In the early 1990s people still relied on paper maps and their own sense of direction to get from point A to point B, which was problem number one for us. We had no paper maps of the island, and none of us had even a modicum of ability to navigate from place to place.

Problem number two for us was the jeep we were driving. It was old and on its last legs. As I pulled out and floored the gas pedal, the first thing I noticed was that the fifteen-year-old jeep had absolutely no pickup. I had to downshift into first gear just to make it over the many hills we were encountering on our way to Orient Beach. We went up one hill after another, barely making it to the apex of the hills before we realized we were lost.

We had absolutely no idea where we were or in what direction we were even heading. Of course, knowing the direction we were heading in wouldn't have really helped, because we didn't have a clue where Orient Beach was located. The man from the rental company had given us directions, but because we were lost, we had long since stopped following those directions.

We kept going up hill after hill, in hopes we'd recognize some landmark that would give us an idea of where we were and how to get to our destination.

Then the unthinkable happened. After I had downshifted to first gear and was trying to navigate up yet another hill, the jeep couldn't make it to the top of this particularly steep hill. The jeep started going backwards down the hill, but I couldn't control the direction it was going. Instead of drifting back in a straight line, it was veering to the right, where the edge of the cliff was.

At the bottom of the cliff was lots of water. Since none of

us had any sense of direction, we had no idea if we were on the eastern side or the western side of the island. The water way below could have been the Atlantic Ocean (if we were on the east side) or the Caribbean Sea (if we were on the west side). In any case, if the jeep fell off of the cliff, we really didn't care which body of water we would have drowned in, assuming we didn't get killed by the impact of hitting the water.

There were also a few cars just a hundred yards or so behind us on the same road. As we drifted back on the road, veering toward the cliff and the ocean below, one of the cars honked his horn, apparently worried that we would miss the cliff and run into him. Diana, who was already terrified, then reacted to the honking in a way that I couldn't even begin to imagine.

Just like a scene in *The Exorcist*, Diana's head turned 180 degrees around her body, and she screamed out a litany of curse words that would make a sailor blush. "You #$@*! &#$@! *#$@!%," screamed my wife. "Can't you see we're going to fall off the cliff and drown?"

I was in shock. Diana never curses! She is such a goody-two-shoes when it comes to her language. In fact, she is such a prude that when a TV or movie character curses, she typically turns away or covers her ears.

Hearing Diana curse like that shocked us all. I really think that everyone in the jeep was torn between bursting out in laughter at Diana's tirade or breaking down in tears, thinking we were going to die.

Thankfully, no one had to make that choice because the crisis lasted only a few seconds. I was able to shift the transmission back into first gear and the rickety old jeep slowly began its climb back up the hill. A different car than the one that honked at us, and turned my wife into Linda Blair from *The Exorcist*, pulled next to us to console us.

"Please, just tell us how to get to Orient Beach," I pleaded.

I received the directions and proceeded to find my way to the place we worked so hard to find. As it turned out, the beach was only about a mile from the ship and should have been easy to find.

However, the nude beach was not the panacea we thought it would be. It was filled with middle-aged people, very few of whom were in good shape. Steve, Jay, and I had thought that watching the nude women would be titillating. It was anything but. After watching these middle-aged men and women walk around without their clothes on, I wanted to yell, "Please get dressed."

Watching the nudists made me realize the real reason clothes were invented—not for warmth but to hide our bodies. We stayed at the beach less than an hour before we headed back to the ship with a story we would remember for the rest of our lives.

Chapter 19

THE LEATHER JACKET

$\mathcal{I}$n the late 1980s and early 1990s, at about the same time that Diana and I started traveling on cruise ships, I began traveling quite a bit as part of my responsibilities at NIST.

NIST provides standards and tests and distributes them to the private sector in order to make companies more productive and more competitive with their counterparts in other countries. NIST develops these standards and tests in a wide variety of disciplines. Chemistry, physics, engineering, and fire and building research are just a few of the disciplines with which NIST is involved.

The newest and perhaps the fastest growing discipline for NIST was information technology (IT). IT is the use of computers to store, receive, transmit, and manipulate data and information. IT had been around for a while before it became part of NIST's mission. The term first appeared back in 1958 in an article in the *Harvard Business Review*, but its usage and importance grew dramatically in the 1980s. At its core, information technology is the application of technology to solve business or organizational problems on a broad scale and was a natural new discipline for NIST, to go along with the older disciplines such as chemistry, physics, and the others.

I worked in the Information Technology Lab (ITL) at NIST.

During the 1990s I was the manager of the Computer Graphics Group within ITL. Computer graphics is the technology of generating images by using computers and is one of the most influential disciplines in the development, advancement, and promulgation of technologies we now take for granted. Digital photography, cell phones, video games, and computer displays are just some of the applications made relevant by computer graphics.

But in the 1990s, these applications were not yet commonplace, even though the discipline of computer graphics had been around since the early 1960s. One of the main barriers to the use of computer graphics applications was the lack of standards to interchange data among computer graphics applications and users of these applications.

The Computer Graphics Group within NIST was chartered to provide standards and tests to interchange data and thus enable the private sector to develop viable computer graphics applications.

As manager of this group, in addition to developing standards for these advanced technologies, my role also involved an ability to 'sell' our products to the companies that needed them. By *sell* I don't mean that the government charged companies for the standards and tests we developed. On the contrary, NIST gives those out for free. However, we had to "sell" those companies on the value of NIST and convince them to use our free products.

It was with this thought in mind that I devised my strategy. I would go to large computer graphics conferences and trade shows to help accomplish these objectives. At the conferences I would typically give a presentation on the work we were doing. This presentation was very technical; thus the audiences for these types of presentations usually consisted of the computer "nerds" who develop the technical products for their company. These "nerds" were computer scientists, computer programmers, and information technology specialists, and it was important to convince our technical counterparts in the private sector that our Computer Graphics Group was developing technically sound products. NIST was a technical organization, and our technical reputation was of great importance.

However, it was equally and perhaps even more important to meet with a different private sector constituency—the managers who made the decisions regarding the goals and direction of their company. These managers were the people to whom I needed to "sell" our products.

I worked diligently on making contacts with various high-level people at these technology companies. My strategy was essentially a two-pronged strategy: 1) Make technical presentations to large audiences at conferences and then 2) follow up on these presentations in the next day or two by meeting high-level managers of IT companies in much smaller groups.

One of main conferences I attended to implement this strategy was a conference called SIGGRAPH. SIGRAPH stands for **S**pecial **I**nterest **G**roup on Computer **Graph**ics and Interactive Techniques and is the premier conference and exhibition in the United States in computer graphics.

My neighbor, Steve Roth, lived across the street from me and also attended SIGGRAPH every year. Steve and I didn't have much in common. But the one thing we did have in common was a love of leather jackets. We both had a large collections of leather jackets. We would often go shopping together in search of good deals on them.

I could never figure out why Steve attended SIGGRAPH. He worked for the Food and Drug Administration and ran the Graphics Arts shop at one of the Food and Drug Administration centers in Rockville, Maryland. In this capacity, Steve created colorful handouts and slides for others to use. Technically, graphics artists do use computer graphics to create illustrations, logos, and graphics that communicate specific messages to a designated audience; however, SIGGRAPH was and still is a technical conference for computer scientists with an emphasis on technical discussions about research and development in the field. You don't have to understand the science behind computer graphics in order to use it to create graphical illustrations.

Sending a user of computer graphics, like Steve, to a conference that accentuates computer graphics research is a bit like sending baseball pitchers to a conference on the science of why a curve ball, thrown by a pitcher, actually curves—interesting but completely unnecessary for the pitcher to do his job. The pitcher needs to know only how to grip the baseball and how to throw it, not why the laws of physics make it curve. Graphics artists need to know only which computer graphics tools to use and how to use these tools to produce the handouts and slides; they do not need to understand the science behind why the tools work.

Perhaps the fact that the locations of SIGRAPH conference were at beautiful and interesting cities like San Diego, New Orleans, Los Angeles, or San Francisco had something to do with Steve's decision to attend.

In July 2000 SIGGRAPH was held in New Orleans and was attended by almost 26,000 participants. Just six months prior to July 2000, I had been promoted to Division Chief of the Software Division, which included, among other things, my old Computer Graphics Group. My new boss, however, was skeptical about many of the projects in our division and in no uncertain terms asked me to produce evidence that our products were used and appreciated by the private sector.

I left for the airport on the Sunday before the meeting and boarded the plane to New Orleans. My neighbor, Steve, was sitting next to me. Steve, of course would not miss a chance to party in the Big Easy, so he was also on his way to this conference.

"I heard they have some great deals on leather jackets in New Orleans," Steve said.

I didn't reply. I was too absorbed in studying the presentation I was going to give to thousands of people at SIGGRAPH.

Like I had been doing for many years, I gave that technical presentation about our research in computer graphics early in the week to the thousands of techies in attendance at SIGGRAPH. The presentation took place in a large auditorium that was supplemented by numerous large TV screens placed outside the auditorium, for attendees who couldn't get into the sold-out auditorium.

After the presentation, I contacted a few important executives in the industry to schedule a small but very important meeting later in the week, with seven or eight vice presidents from companies that were giants in the IT arena: Microsoft, Apple, and IBM, among others. I reserved a room at the conference to give presentations on the division's work and to "sell" the VPs on the importance of the products we wanted to give them for free. My division consisted of three groups, and I brought all three Group Managers along with me to this make-or-break meeting. The stakes could not have been higher.

My group managers and I were tense, but the meeting was going quite well. We had made a few presentations, and I was finishing the last presentation before beginning the crucial task of trying to get the VIPs to get onboard with our work and, I hoped, write letters of support to both my boss and the NIST Director.

Just as I began speaking about my last slide, I heard a knock at the door.

"Who could this be?" I thought. I had reserved the room for the whole morning, and I still had two hours left.

I heard the knock again.

"Excuse me," I said to my guests and went to open the door.

My neighbor, Steve, burst in, excited and out of breadth.

"What's wrong?" I said, fearing the worst.

"Mark, I have to speak to you."

"Okay. Let's go outside."

We left the room when Steve, to my amazement, said, "Mark, you won't believe this leather jacket I just bought."

"What?" I said, incredulous.

"It's the nicest leather jacket I've ever seen. It's black, but the arms are brown. The contrast is the coolest thing I've ever seen."

"But Steve, as I told you the other day, this is the most important meeting of my career. My job depends on it."

"I know, but once you see this leather jacket, you'll understand."

I took a deep breath and tried to stay calm. "Okay. I'll come look at it after our meeting is finished."

"You don't understand. You have to come now. They're almost sold out."

"Okay, then why don't you pick one up for me, and I'll pay you back?"

"I can't do that. The jackets run a little small, so you'll have to try them on. You have to come with me now."

"I'll take my chances, Steve! I'll look at them later!"

Steve finally left and I returned to my meeting. The rest of the presentations went very well, and we ended with a commitment from all the companies to use our products.

After lunch, I decided to take a walk to the store selling the leather jackets that got my friend so excited.

"Can I help you sir?" asked the salesman as I walked in the door.

"I'm looking for a leather jacket that's black with brown sleeves," I said to the man.

"Follow me, sir. We have an exceptionally large selection of those jackets."

I walked to the end of the store, where at least thirty of the black-and-brown-leather jackets were hanging. The contrast of the jacket sleeves in a different color reminded me of my favorite blue mohair sweater with different-color sleeves that Aunt Esther knitted for me when I was a teenager. That sweater almost got me killed when my girlfriend, Estelle, and I were accosted by a street gang back when I lived in Brooklyn.

I tried on one of the leather jackets. It fit me perfectly, and I took out my credit card to pay the man.

"Good choice, sir. I think you'll like the jacket, although I don't understand why they're not selling. In fact, a man came in earlier today and bought the first one we sold all month."

So much for Steve urging me to leave my meeting immediately because the jackets were almost sold out.

Despite all the turmoil surrounding this purchase, I really did like the jacket. To this day I still own it and wear it. The leather jacket that I bought in New Orleans hangs proudly in my closet right next to my blue mohair sweater.

Chapter 20

IT'S JUST A FANTASY

During my years at NIST I worked extremely hard. But I played hard too. I loved sports and I played many sports. My favorites were basketball and tennis, each of which I played about twice a week.

I also watched many sports, both in person and on television. I followed my original New York teams, like the Mets in baseball and the Giants in football, but for some strange reason I had become a Washington Capitals fan in hockey and a Washington Bullets (later Wizards) fan in basketball.

Diana and I were season ticket holders for the Capitals, so we went to many hockey games in person. I also traveled to New York to see a few Met games every year. Once or twice a decade I was lucky enough to get a ticket to a New York Football Giants game, and I traveled to New Jersey (where the Giants had moved their stadium) to watch them play.

And of course I watched as many games as I could on TV. I would often invite friends over to watch Met games on television (in the summer) and Giants games (in the winter). But even when games weren't being played, my friends and I would talk about sports incessantly. We would argue about which players we liked and who was better than whom.

I would always use statistics to make my point about why I

thought one player was better than another. I was up to date on the batting averages, home run totals, earned-run averages, and wins of my favorite players in baseball and completion percentage, yards per carry, yards per reception, and touchdowns of my favorite football players.

I would use these statistics to talk about baseball or football with everyone I knew and some who I didn't.

One day, I had just boarded a plane to go on another one of my business trips. Serendipitously, I was seated next to another man who was studying a notebook with what seemed to contain a slew of statistics about baseball players. He was also looking at a newspaper that had box scores of the previous day's games.

"Excuse me," I said. "Can I ask what you're doing with all of that data about baseball players?"

"Sure, no problem," he responded. "I'm compiling statistics for all of the teams in our fantasy baseball league."

"Fantasy what?" I responded.

"Fantasy baseball."

I certainly knew all about baseball and a little bit about fantasy, but I had never conceived that the two would be merged.

"Pray tell, what is fantasy baseball?"

"It's a game where people draft teams consisting of players from the list of all existing major league baseball players. Then every time one of the hitters gets a hit or hits a home run or a pitcher gets a strikeout or a win, you use those statistics for each player on your team and then add up all the statistics to see how your whole team performed in a number of categories."

I was instantly hooked. I loved statistics and I loved baseball, so how could I not love a game that anyone could play that combined both baseball and statistics?

I researched the game and found out that fantasy baseball, sometimes called rotisserie baseball, was developed in the 1980s by a group of journalists who called the league the Rotisserie Baseball League, named after the New York City restaurant La Rotisserie Francaise, where its founders met for lunch and formed the first fantasy baseball league. Traditional statistics, like batting average and home runs for hitters and wins and earned averages for pitchers, were chosen because they were easy to compile from newspaper box scores.

The advent of powerful computers and the internet eventually led to these statistics being compiled entirely by computers, but in its early years these statistics were painfully compiled by hand by league "commissioners" like the fellow sitting next to me.

After I returned from my business trip, I called my son, Howard, and proposed that he and I form a fantasy baseball league. He quickly agreed. We formed a league consisting of Howard's friends and my friends. There were eight teams in the league, and we all enjoyed the camaraderie of getting together to draft the teams every year, as well as the competitiveness of trying to beat our friends and win the league championship.

The same league continued for four or five years in a row, after which one of the team members decided he did not want to continue being in the league anymore.

I was the league commissioner at that time and thus had the responsibility of finding a new team owner to replace the one that left. I took this job very seriously, because I loved fantasy baseball and I did not want the league to fold because we didn't have enough teams. By early March of that year, I had not yet successfully recruited a new team owner, and the major league baseball season was beginning in just a few weeks. I was really feeling the pressure.

One night we were out to dinner with our neighbors Steve and Sue, and I casually mentioned the pressure I was feeling to get a new team owner for our league.

"I have a great idea," said Sue. "I'll be in your league."

"What?" I said.

"What?" said her husband, Steve, of leather jacket fame.

"Well, Sue, you know, there are no women in our league, only men," I reminded her.

"That's okay. I think this will be good for Steve. He doesn't really follow sports, and if I'm in the league, it might get him interested in baseball."

"But this has to be a definite commitment," I responded. "There are only a few weeks left before the season starts, and our draft will be held the day before that. You can't change your mind after you commit."

"I'm in," said Sue. "Once I give a commitment, I never break my word."

"Are you sure?" I asked.

"I'm sure."

"But you can't change your mind once you commit," I repeated again.

"I'm in, and I'm sure."

I'm a bit obsessive-compulsive, and I wanted to be absolutely sure that our league would not be missing a team owner come the first game of the baseball season and our fantasy draft, so I called Sue every day or two just to remind her that she could not back out of her commitment.

Every time, she assured me that she was a woman of her word. "I'm in," she said repeatedly. "You can count on it. My word is my bond."

Then about four days before our scheduled draft, the phone rang. My caller ID told me that Sue was calling.

I knew instantly why she was calling me.

"Mark, I can't do it," said Sue. "There was so much male testosterone in all of the emails that went back and forth."

"What about, you can't back out once you commit, didn't you understand?" I was trying, but failing, to control my emotions.

"I'm sorry. I just can't do it."

I hung up half in shock. I spent the next day calling just about every person I knew, begging them to join our league. I finally got my good friend Stan Willner to take over the team Sue owned for three whole weeks. As it turned out Stan was a terrific team owner, and he and I battled it out for many championships over the years.

But I never forgot this incident, and to this day, almost every time I see Sue, I remind her of how she almost made our league break up. She has gotten over it. I have not.

Fantasy sports leagues weren't, and still aren't, relegated to just baseball. Fantasy leagues sprung up for almost all the other major sports, including football, basketball, and hockey.

The year after forming our fantasy baseball league, the same group of friends formed a fantasy football league. Fantasy football was a little different from fantasy baseball, but both fantasy sports used categories of production particular to their sport. Whereas baseball used batting average, home runs, earned-run average, and wins, among other categories, fantasy football categories centered on touchdowns, yardage gained, field goals, and extra points made.

Our fantasy football league was extremely competitive and just as much fun as our fantasy baseball league.

I loved competing in all the fantasy leagues. But, after just a year or two of fantasy sports, an unanticipated problem arose.

I loved the New York Football Giants, and I rooted for them with all of my energy. But now I became the fantasy coach/general manager of a team of players, most of whom were players from other teams in the league. When those players from other teams scored touchdowns, including touchdowns against my beloved New York Giants, it dramatically helped my fantasy team.

So, when watching the Giants play against a team that had one or more of my fantasy players on that team, whom and what did I root for?

I certainly couldn't root against the Giants. On the other hand, I am incredibly competitive and really wanted to beat the owners of the other fantasy teams in our league. People would ask me how much money I won when I won a fantasy league championship. Fantasy league champions did indeed win money, but much more importantly we won bragging rights. A few hundred dollars paled in comparison to having our names on the championship trophy and the right to "talk trash" to the other team owners.

Thus when watching Giants games, I adopted the strategy of rooting for the Giants to win the game but also rooting for my fantasy players on the opposing team to do well. But during every Giants game, every time one of the opposing players on my fantasy team did well, like when they scored a touchdown, it decreased the odds of the Giants winning the game. What a conundrum. This was a real Catch-22.

Most of my friends in Maryland originally came from New York and were Giant fans. Many were also the guys in my fantasy league. My friends and I, as well as Howard and his friends who were Giants fans, typically went to a "Giants" bar every Sunday to watch the Giants play.

Every time a Giants player made a nice play or scored a touchdown, we would all instinctively cheer. However, I would also secretly be rooting for my fantasy players on the other team to do well, even though it hurt the Giants. Again, I was hoping my players would do well, but the Giants would still win. Thus when one of my fantasy players on the opposing team did well, and especially when they scored a touchdown, I would cheer, but it was a silent cheer.

I would cheer silently because I never wanted to let on to my friends and my son, all of whom were as fanatical as I was about the Giants, that I would even think about rooting for anything that was detrimental to the Giants. As opposed to me, I think that almost all the other Giants fans in our fantasy league placed all of their rooting interest in the Giants and none on their fantasy team, when it came to their players playing against the Giants.

Then one day, while watching a Giants game with my friends, the unthinkable happened. It was the last week of the season and I was in first place in our fantasy league, but another team was quickly gaining ground on me. This was a must-win game for my fantasy team.

One of my fantasy running backs on the team playing against the Giants scored a touchdown, and I jumped up and started cheering, and not in a silent way! I was so embarrassed. I sat down quickly and made believe that nothing strange had happened.

"I didn't mean that," I said sheepishly.

"Yeah, sure," my friend John said and looked at me with disdain.

I was embarrassed and humiliated. I had shown myself to be an unworthy Giants fan in front of my son and many of my friends. Once this story got out, I was sure to be scorned by true Giant fans everywhere and treated as a traitor. And all because of fantasy football!

Chapter 21

IT'S A LONG WALK

The team owners of the first fantasy football league that Howard and I were in were friends of mine from NIST and friends of Howard's. But since we were having so much fun in this league, after a few years we decided to join a second fantasy football league.

This second league was being formed by a colleague of Howard's, and neither Howard nor I knew any of the other people in the league.

We met all the other team owners at the first fantasy football league draft that we had for this new league.

The fantasy draft is where all team owners get together to select the players who will be on their team. For our first fantasy football league, we got together at people's houses. We rotated houses every year among all of the team owners.

However, for the new fantasy football league, we met at Hooters, the somewhat infamous restaurant chain. In fact, the name of our league was called Hooters.

The wait staff at Hooters consisted primarily of young women whose revealing outfits and sex appeal were played up and were a primary component of the company's image. I liked young, sexy women as much as the next guy, but I had never been to Hooters before this new fantasy football league was formed. In fact, I had always thought that the men who frequented that bar/restaurant were degenerates and dirty old men.

After meeting the rest of our league for the first time at Hooters, it turns out I was right.

At the draft we ordered so many pitchers of beer that Hooters had to assign additional waitresses to our table. However, having so many young, scantily clad women serving these guys turned out to be a big mistake.

Almost all the team owners got drunk and flirted with the waitresses. Some of the things they said were pretty obnoxious. In fact, it was a miracle that we were able to finish our draft before anyone got thrown out of the restaurant.

But the full extent of these guys' somewhat questionable personalities wasn't revealed until a week or so later after the first week of football had been played and the first week's standings of the Hooters league was put up on our website.

Sometimes men, especially pro athletes playing sports like to "talk trash" during the games. This trash talking often involves disparaging, taunting, boastful comments to members of the other team to try to intimidate the opponent. Sometimes the trash talking can get personal and insulting.

Since fantasy sports can be an extension of real sports, trash talking can occur between team owners there as well. However, in fantasy sports, the trash talking is usually lighthearted and funny.

But not when guys from our new fantasy football league were involved.

During those days, I used my work email to send and receive personal email, including emails pertaining to my fantasy leagues, but as it turned out, that was a big mistake.

The first email sent out by a team owner was to another team owner, but he copied the whole league on the email. It went something like this: "While I was watching my team destroy your team, I was also "f*ck*n* your sister. Then your mother walked in."

In all fairness the email was intended to be lighthearted and funny, but I certainly didn't want anybody at NIST to see this email. I quickly got a separate email account and used this personal account for all email chains for the Hooters league.

Many years later when my daughter, Staci, became a big football and fantasy football fan, she asked to join our Hooters league. I explained to her that it really wasn't for women, since the men were disgustingly crude. I sent her that profane email from the first year.

She countered by saying, "C'mon, Dad. I'm your daughter. I've seen and heard a lot worse."

I couldn't argue with that. Later, Staci joined our league and the league name got changed to Hooters Chick and Dicks.

Besides drafting players, team owners could also acquire players for their fantasy teams by trading with other team owners.

I would get a slew of trade proposals from other team owners. Most of them were reasonable offers, but some were completely unreasonable, where another team wanted to trade a mediocre player and wanted a superstar from my team in return.

Although most of the Hooters team owners took the league very seriously, one of the team owners barely knew who was on his team. It was pretty obvious that he joined the league just to come to the draft, get drunk, and ogle the waitresses at Hooters.

But his son, who was only twelve years old at the time, was really interested in fantasy football and made all the decisions for his father concerning whom to draft. He also made trade proposals for his dad's team. Since he was so young, he didn't realize that, for a trade to work, both teams had to receive players that would make their teams better. As with most kids, he thought others should give him things for practically nothing.

One day I received a trade proposal from this twelve-year-old. It fell into the completely unreasonable category; however, as I did with all my other fantasy trade proposals, I made a counter-offer in the hopes of negotiating a trade that would help both teams.

I sent a few emails and received a few emails in return from this kid, but then surprisingly, I received an email from his mother.

"Sorry, but it's past Ben's bedtime, and he has to go to sleep. You'll have to continue this discussion tomorrow."

I had received many strange responses in all of my years making trades in fantasy sports, but to be told that it was way past my trading partner's bedtime had to be a first.

Even though Howard and I regularly went to Giants bars to watch the games and to root for our fantasy players, occasionally the Giants game would be televised in Maryland. During those rare instances, Howard and I would stay home and watch the game there. All playoff games were televised nationally, so we would watch those games at home as well.

For the game Howard and I were watching this particular Sunday, our fantasy season was over, and the NFL playoffs were here. Playoff games are the most exciting games for true fans to watch. The New York Football Giants were playing the San Francisco 49ers.

The 49ers were an excellent team, having won five Super Bowls between the years 1981 and 1994. In fact, in 1994, I had been in San Francisco during the Super Bowl because of a business meeting, and I had watched the team's Super Bowl win in a local bar there with hundreds of rabid 49er fans. I had always had a soft spot for the 49ers after watching them win the Super Bowl and celebrating that victory with 49er fans in the city by the Bay.

Howard and I were very excited to watch this playoff game between our Giants and the 49ers in the 2002 playoffs, played on January 5, 2003. We bought pretzels and potato chips, to go along with a case of beer, and settled in to watch the game.

The game started at 4:45, and Diana was long gone by then. She typically disappeared on Sundays around lunchtime and would not return until dinnertime. She usually didn't tell me where she went, but I was quite sure she went to malls and department stores to buy clothes.

"Born to shop" was Diana's motto. My wife's shopping cost me lots of money, but being left watching football undisturbed was priceless.

This playoff game was played in sunny weather in San Francisco, but home in Maryland it was windy, raining, and very nasty outside. In fact the freezing rain was supposed to turn to snow later in the day, but in the comfort of my living room, I didn't care.

The score seesawed back and forth, and the game was very tense. The Giants were ahead 38-22 at the end of the third quarter.

Howard and I were completely absorbed in the game, so much so, that we never realized that Diana, who is usually home by dinnertime, had not yet returned home. We also hadn't noticed that quite a few inches of snow were covering the streets.

We still were not aware of Diana's delay when we watched the 49ers score seventeen unanswered points in the fourth quarter and beat the Giants 39-38.

Howard and I were heartbroken.

We had a lengthy discussion about how any team, especially our beloved Giants, could blow a 17-point lead in such an important game.

Then the doorbell rang.

It was Diana.

"Oh my God, she hadn't come home by now," I thought as soon I answered the door. Something horrific must have happened.

She looked terrible. Her hair was soaking wet, and she was shivering from the cold. Also, she was covered in snow.

"'What happened?" I asked.

"My car got a flat tire in the Muddy Branch Shopping Center," she said. "It was Sunday and none of the gas stations were fixing flats, so I left the car there and walked home. I left all my packages in the trunk of the car."

Muddy Branch Shopping Center was about a mile and a half from our house.

"Why didn't you call me to come pick you up?" I asked.

"I knew you were watching the Giants game and you would never leave in the middle of the game, especially a playoff game," she responded matter-of-factly.

I've never been prouder of my wife!

Chapter 22

AM I PASSIONATE ENOUGH?

*M*y years working for NIST were a great source of satisfaction for me. I did remarkably interesting and important work and I performed this work alongside brilliant and very likeable people. In addition I got to travel to many great places. I was the NIST representative to the World Wide Web Consortium (W3C) and attended the consortium meetings chaired by Tim Berners-Lee. The World Wide Web and the internet are often used interchangeably, but they are not the same. The internet forms the foundation for the web to function. The internet is a global system of interconnected networks, while the web is a global collection of documents available on the internet. The web and the internet are codependent—one would lose its value without the other. Vinton Cerf and Bob Kahn invented the internet (no, it was not Al Gore), while Tim Berners-Lee invented the World Wide Web.

The World Wide Web is accessed by users via a software application called a browser. Common browsers include Microsoft Explorer, Microsoft Edge, Chrome, and Safari. These browsers are currently available on desktop computers, laptop computers, smart phones, and tablets.

However, when I was attending W3C meetings and the standards for the web were being developed, none of these browsers existed. Besides inventing the World Wide Web, Tim Berners-Lee also wrote the first web browser in 1990. The World Wide Web has been central to the development of the Information Age and is the primary tool that billions of people use to interact on the internet. Websites made possible by the World Wide Web provide a myriad of informative, entertainment, commercial, and governmental applications.

Because of his pioneering work, Tim Berners-Lee was named one of *Time Magazine's* 100 most important people of the 20th century. Tim Berners-Lee is a British citizen and in 2004 was knighted by Queen Elizbeth II in recognition of his "services to the global development of the internet."

Working with one of the pioneers of our industry was a great honor for me. I not only got to work with Sir TBL, as we called him, but also the meetings were held in a fabulous location. We met twice a year in a little town in France called Valbonne. Valbonne is a small city in southeastern France on the French Riviera, in between Nice and Cannes.

During our free time after meetings, or sometimes on our days off, W3C participants got to explore beautiful nearby towns such as Saint-Tropez and Monte Carlo. I was able to lose money in the luxurious casinos in Monte Carlo. When I had no money left, I was fortunate enough to drive my rented government car around the streets of Monte Carlo on the same exact route used by the Formula 1 Grand Prix racers. Not a bad way to spend two weeks every year.

Making history by allowing the World Wide Web to prosper while at the same time, traveling to one of the most beautiful spots in the world was both greatly satisfying and exhilarating.

Besides Valbonne I traveled to other exotic locations, like London, Paris, Munich, and Austria, to attend standards meetings, give presentations, and consult with colleagues.

I thoroughly enjoyed my years at NIST, but by 2008, after I had worked forty-two years in the federal government, my enthusiasm began to wane. I still enjoyed the challenging research and the exciting business trips, but the federal government bureaucracy was getting me down.

I've always been an employee who is very frank. I respect my superiors and I never speak to them in a rude or condescending manner. But I speak my mind. If I'm asked a question by one of my bosses, I'm going to give him or her my honest opinion. In fact often times, even when I'm not asked for my opinion, I will tell my bosses what I think about their goals or plans for the organization, when I disagree with those goals or plans.

It was becoming more and more difficult to sit at management meetings and listen to my boss say something that was either not factually true or with which I passionately disagreed.

When hearing something I considered completely wrong, I was faced with two alternatives. Either I could sit stoically and say nothing or I could respectfully "correct" my boss and explain why his or her proposal would be disastrous for NIST. Neither alternative left me feeling good afterwards.

If I did not speak up, I felt like I had not performed my job properly. How could I allow something that I knew was incorrect to continue to move forward and possibly do harm to the organization?

Conversely, if I did speak up, I knew that my insecure boss would get terribly upset and continue to argue with me, either during the meeting or sometimes later, behind closed doors.

"I respectfully disagree," would be my usual response. I would then go on to explain why I felt that way. In my world, all opinions needed to be justified by citing the facts.

Rather than receiving a factual counterargument, "Do you think I'm a dumb dispshit?" was one of the responses I received from my boss during one of these exchanges. To me, the issue was not whether or not my boss agreed with me or adopted my proposal. It was my boss's decision to make, and he or she would make it. I just wanted the conversation to be logical and to be based on the facts.

Now, I'm not naïve enough to believe that everyone is logical and that everything happens the way it should. I know that everyone has bosses that they disagree with and that much of the time workers think that their boss is illogical.

I get it.

In fact I'd been dealing with bosses like this my whole career. I didn't like it, but I accepted it.

Until I didn't accept it.

I'm not sure why, but during that last year or so, it became more and more difficult to put up with this.

I ran a large division that did important work, and perhaps, as we got closer and closer to achieving our goals, I just didn't want a random decision to derail the work. Perhaps I didn't want to let down the many smart and dedicated people in my division.

Or perhaps I had just run out of patience.

The thought of retiring from the federal government had become more and more enticing to me. After forty-two years I had maxed out my government pension, so continuing to work was not economically all that profitable. By retiring I would receive about 80 percent of my salary to sit home and do nothing.

So I decided to retire.

Right after making that decision, I signed up for a retirement class offered by NIST.

The first day of the class was predictable and boring. It was taught by a financial analyst. I'm a numbers guy, and I had already done the math to figure out how to handle my pension, my life insurance, and all other financial decisions. Even so, having the retirement specialist reassure me that my decisions were on point had a calming effect on me.

Then we got to the second day. The second day's subject matter really intrigued me. It was taught by a psychologist. This discussion was intended to examine the psychological issues associated with retirement. My daughter, Staci, had grown up to become a (school) psychologist, and I had always had an interest in the field of psychology.

The psychologist started the day by explaining how to go about figuring out where to live after retiring. He explained that many people who retire relocate to an area where they had gone on vacation. He cautioned against this inclination and explained that spending a week or two at an area while vacationing and spending a lifetime there are two vastly different things. He recommended renting a place for a few months in an area where you're considering retiring. In that way, you can see what it's like to live, rather than to play, in a new location. Good advice, I thought.

Next, the psychologist discussed the worrisome psychological aspects of retirement. "Many people get sad after retirement, and they get very depressed. They often become manic depressives and sometimes even become suicidal," the psychologist said.

Everybody sat very still.

"Unless you have a passion," he continued. "Without a passion, retirees get bored and then become depressed. You have to have a passion!"

The instructor then went around the room and asked each of us to tell everyone else in the class what our passion is.

"I'm going to volunteer at hospitals and help the sick, especially ones in the final stages of their illnesses," said the soft-spoken woman in the corner of the room. "I've always wanted to do this, and after retirement, I'll finally have the time."

"That's great," said the psychologist.

"I'm going to open up my own business," said a large gentleman in the center of the room. "I've worked for the government my whole life, and I've had many ideas that I couldn't pursue. I can finally try out all the different ideas I've had, and I'm hoping this passion of mine can also make me rich."

"Sounds very intriguing," said the psychologist.

"I've always been interested in education," said the fellow next to me. "In fact when I was young, I was going to be a teacher, but it just wouldn't pay enough for me to be able to support my family. Now that I have enough money, I can do what I've always dreamed about doing my whole life."

"I think you'll find that will be very fulfilling," said the psychologist.

Next it was my turn to speak. "Does sleeping until noon and playing fantasy baseball and fantasy football count?" I asked sheepishly.

"Sir, never retire!" said the psychologist.

Everybody looked at me.

But I retired anyway.

After retirement I, of course, spent more time preparing for and playing in my fantasy sports leagues, but I also ended up performing contracts for the federal government and writing this book.

With all the additional free time that I had, I was able to study for fantasy drafts in my usual compulsive fashion. To this day I continue to win a lot of fantasy leagues, not because I'm smarter than my competitors, but because I outwork them. Outworking people takes time, and I now have the time. Thanks to retirement.

Chapter 23

LET'S VOTE ON THAT

*I*n the last several years of my career, right before I retired, my work had taken on a whole different emphasis. I had become the number-one expert, perhaps in the whole country, on elections. I was in charge of developing standards and tests for voting machines used in federal and state elections.

The genesis of this new work began in 2002, when Congress passed the Help America Vote Act (HAVA) in direct response to the controversy surrounding the 2000 election of George Bush over Al Gore, when almost two million ballots were disqualified because they registered no votes or sometimes registered multiple votes when run through vote-counting machines. Who will ever forget the "hanging chads" fiasco?

HAVA charged NIST with developing Voluntary Voting System Guidelines (VVSG) that were to be distributed to all fifty states and units of local government for their use. The VVSG was a huge step forward in getting elections to be accurate, secure, and usable, as well as accessible to disabled people. HAVA also created the Election Assistance Commission (EAC), a new federal government agency, to create and maintain the VVSG.

HAVA assigned NIST the task of providing research and establishing the technical standards and tests that are needed.

At the beginning of this effort by NIST, I was only peripherally involved. I was the division chief of a large division, and I was very busy.

But this all changed suddenly.

Sometime in early 2004 I was sitting at my desk, minding my own business, when the NIST director, Hratch Semerjian, called me into his office. Like a child being summoned into the principal's office, I was worried. I knew the NIST director slightly. Most of my dealings with Hratch had involved a few technical presentations that I had given to keep him up to date on various subjects that were likely to arise when he met with his boss, the Secretary of Commerce. I had also met with him once on a personnel matter that involved one of my subordinates.

But I certainly had never been summoned to the director's office.

I entered Dr. Semerjian's office with much trepidation.

"Hello, Mark. How are you?" asked Hratch Semerjian, who was only the acting, rather than the permanent, NIST director but still carried a lot of clout and was very well respected but also universally feared.

"I'm fine."

"Well, Mark, I have good news and bad news," said Hratch. "The good news is don't worry; you're not in trouble."

I breathed a sigh of relief.

"And the bad news?"

"The bad news is that from now on you will be reporting directly to me," Hratch joked. "I'm putting you in charge of the NIST voting project."

I was in shock and not happy. I had a great job heading the Software Division, and I didn't want to give it up. "With all due respect, Dr. Semerjian, I love the work I'm doing now. I would hate to give that up."

"Don't worry, Mark. You don't have to give that work up. You can do both jobs."

"Great. Do I get two paychecks?" I joked.

The stare that Hratch Semerjian gave me led me to believe that perhaps the acting NIST director did not share my sense of humor.

But it all worked out. My work leading the NIST voting project turned out to be the most rewarding work I had ever done in my career. Additionally I ended up having an excellent working relationship with Hratch, as well as with his successor, Bill Jeffrey, who succeeded Hratch as the permanent NIST director.

In my new job I got to meet hundreds of dedicated voting officials, the Secretaries of State of most of our fifty states, and many congressmen and senators. I testified on Capitol Hill numerous times and once testified at City Hall in New York in front of then freshman Senator Kirsten Gillibrand, who would eventually go on to become a Democratic presidential candidate in 2020.

I was the person responsible for the development of the Voluntary Voting System Guidelines. My team and I were doing detailed technical work, and the resulting guidelines were also incredibly detailed. During the development of these guidelines, I had to present them at many different levels to many different types of people. Some of these people were very technical, while others had no technical background whatsoever. I initially presented these guidelines to computer scientists in order to obtain feedback regarding their correctness. NIST certainly couldn't afford for these guidelines to be technically incorrect, and we thus sought advice from the best technical minds we could find.

But later on, I had to present these guidelines to the politicians with whom I had liaised. This included the Secretaries of State and quite a few people from Congress. Since these guidelines were so technical, they were difficult for laymen to understand. They were especially difficult for politicians to understand.

Politicians typically have their staffers break down detailed technical issues into easily understandable chunks and then have these chunks presented to them in a much more general and understandable manner. However, no matter how much they tried, many of these staffers were not able to communicate to their bosses the difficult technical issues addressed in the voting guidelines.

The task then fell upon me to present these technical guidelines at a much more general level, in a way that was understandable to the politicians. This was not an easy job, and it didn't always go well. I had serious run-ins with some of the Secretaries that included a few shouting matches. But the work was exhilarating, and I even enjoyed the back and forth with the politicians. I loved the challenge, and ended up successfully presenting the VVSG to the Secretaries of State of all fifty states and to several members of Congress.

I also had a lot of fun doing this work. Besides high-level politicians, I also worked with lower-level state voting officials. The state voting officials that I worked with on a day-to-day basis were dedicated civil servants. They were overworked, very conscientious, and very stressed. They had to relieve the stress somehow. Often it was at the bar right after their meetings.

Right after the state voting officials explained the difficult nature of their job, the lack of resources provided to them, and the unreasonable timelines imposed on them, it became apparent to me that they had an almost impossible job to do. No wonder they were so stressed. They jokingly told me that alcoholism was an occupational hazard of the voting profession.

After many of our meetings that I had with the voting officials, I would accompany them to the bar. After all, this new job that I was doing, on top of my day job as division chief of the

Software Division, was stressful to me as well. I got to know my new colleagues very well in this social setting. I can't say that I remember any of the details from those post-meeting get-togethers, but I know that they were fun, and they definitely relieved stress.

NIST and the EAC were meeting with many of these same election officials in New Orleans during a hot August week in 2004. After the meeting a few of us went to Pat O'Brien's to drink Hurricanes.

Pat O'Brien's is a bar located in the French Quarter in New Orleans and was built around the turn of the nineteenth century. Pat O'Brien's is reported to have invented the Hurricane cocktail in the 1940s. Legend has it that since scotch was difficult to import during World War II, liquor salesmen forced bar owners to buy as many as fifty cases of their much more plentiful rum, in order to get a single case of scotch. To utilize all that rum, the bartenders at O'Briens came up with a great-tasting recipe for the rum. When they decided to serve it in a glass shaped like a hurricane lamp, the Hurricane drink was born.

I was sitting in the courtyard at Pat O'Briens sipping my Hurricane along with Tom Hicks, who was one of the EAC commissioners. The EAC commissioners were political appointees and had to be confirmed by Congress. The commissioners were usually very boring and very conventional. Not Tom Hicks. He was good at his job and very professional when he needed to be, but he certainly knew how to have a good time.

Tom Hicks and I were joined by Matt Masterson, a good friend and colleague of mine from the EAC, some other people from the EAC, and a few voting officials. As we were sitting in the courtyard and sipping our drinks, we overheard a young couple arguing. Apparently, they were engaged to be married but had just decided to call off the wedding. Tom and I, feeling no pain, walked over to them to talk to them while the rest of our group cheered us on. The conversation lasted a long time. Yada yada yada, the marriage was back on! We were all immensely proud of ourselves. We made elections better, and in our spare time, we also saved people's marriages.

After we left Pat O'Briens, we headed back to our hotel as a group. It was extremely hot and muggy, and I could barely walk because of my newly acquired Hurricane-induced inebriation. I wanted to go into some of the bars on the way back to our hotel to allow the air conditioning to cool me down, but I knew that if I sat down inside the bar, I would never be able to get up. Thus I swung around the poles that were inside the bars, to stop from falling and to propel myself back outside. Later, my colleagues told me that I was so drunk that I was falling into the bars on the way back, but I told them that was my strategy for cooling off. That's my story, and I'm sticking to it!

Chapter 24

NOW THAT'S A SCARY MOVIE

My job had so many highlights. I did leading-edge technical work, worked with legendary technical giants like Tim Berners-Lee, as well as influential politicians at every level, and got to travel to great locations. Plus I was having lots of fun, like at the meeting in New Orleans. So exactly why was I retiring?

I was certainly going to miss the work. Right before I retired, I started having second thoughts. I really loved my job.

I started panicking. Could I really be happy without this job that I loved? That's when I realized that working, as opposed to retiring, did not have to be an either-or situation. That was a false choice. I wanted both and I could have both. I could have my proverbial cake and eat it too! I would continue working, just not for the federal government. I would become a contractor *to* the federal government, as opposed to an employee *of* the federal government.

I would retire but still continue to work. And work at the same things that had made me fall in love with my job at NIST. I just wouldn't have to deal with the bureaucratic nonsense that had made me want to retire in the first place. What a deal!

This would be the ideal solution. Not only could I continue doing a job that I loved, but it would also be very lucrative to be "double dipping," collecting my monthly annuity check from the Office of Personnel Management and another check for my work as an independent contractor.

I thought back to the retirement psychologist telling me that I needed a passion to survive retirement. I realized that perhaps my passion was the work that I had done most of my life. If I continued that work into my retirement years, perhaps I could avoid the dangers of boredom and the subsequent depressions the psychologist had, not so gently, warned us about.

I tried to think about contacts I had made over the years and specifically which ones I could approach about trying to get a contract to continue my work on voting. I needed to set this in motion before I retired, so that I could begin my work as a contractor right after I retired.

I immediately thought about my friend and colleague, Matt Masterson, at the Election Assistance Commission. Matt had come to the EAC from Ohio and had worked directly for the Ohio Secretary of State and had even met on occasion with Governor Kasich. Matt was very smart and a polished speaker. His goal was to go into politics. I nicknamed him The Governor because I really thought he would be one eventually.

The fact that Matt was also in my fantasy baseball league and a good friend didn't hurt my chances of getting a contract from him. I had recruited him into our league a few years back and he aptly named his team The Governors.

I asked him if the EAC would be interested in giving me a contract to help monitor the voting testing laboratories that were testing for adherence to the standard that I had created. Matt thought it was a great idea and immediately went to work to put the contract in place.

I knew from experience that because of the government bureaucracy, there could be a long wait between the time a contract was written and the time it was awarded, so I asked Matt to start putting this contract into place many months before I was scheduled to retire.

"How's the contract coming along, Matt?" I would ask him almost every day, in the weeks and months leading up to my retirement.

"Slowly," he would say.

Finally the day came. On January 9, 2009, I retired from NIST and the federal government. The retirement party was great, and I left NIST that day sad but also excited about what would come next. However, the contract that Matt was working on for me still hadn't been finalized.

The weekend that directly followed my retirement was strange. I had just stopped doing what I had been doing for almost my entire life. I was certainly looking forward to my great new adventure, but I was still a bit apprehensive about how everything would play out.

I was still waiting for my contract to be finalized as the days of the following week slowly dragged on. I really couldn't figure out exactly how to fill up my days. Boredom was already setting in.

On Thursday Diana finally said, "I have a great idea. Let's go to the movies at the Rio Theater."

We hadn't been to the movies in quite a while, and the last time we went to the movies, about six months earlier, it turned out to be one of the most embarrassing moments of my life.

That embarrassing event happened at the very same Rio movie theater that Diana had just suggested we attend. I hadn't even thought about retirement six months earlier. We were in our early sixties, and sixty-something didn't seem that old, but we were beginning to be considered "seniors". One of the only good things about getting old were the senior discounts. Some senior discounts were available for people 55 or older, some for people 62 or older, and some only for people who had reached the ripe old age of 65. Apparently, the definition of a senior varied greatly among different retail outlets. It was difficult enough becoming a senior, but being considered old at some places but not at others confused me. No wonder they say seniors get confused easily.

Since the senior age requirement was confusing and vague, I used the age requirement for seniors to my advantage. In my mind I was still in junior high school playing stickball, so I certainly didn't feel like a senior; however, when purchasing something where senior discounts were available, I always asked for the discount.

Movie theaters were giving discounts on their tickets to seniors. I did not know for certain what definition movie theaters used to define seniors, but somewhere in the back of my mind, I thought I had read on one of the ticket stubs that movie theaters were using the "very old man" definition of 65.

In any case, I really didn't think it mattered. It was certainly in the spirit, if not the letter, of the law for me to purchase a senior ticket to the movies. Plus, almost all of the ushers and ticket takers in movie theaters were kids. There was no way an 18-year-old could even discern the difference between a 50-year-old and a 70-year-old, much less noticing that I was 62 rather than 65.

Diana and I walked to the Rio Theater ticket booth on a warm Saturday night sometime in the summer of 2008, six months before my retirement.

"We'd like two senior tickets, please," I said.

"Certainly," said the young woman behind the ticket booth. "Enjoy the show."

But then a strange thing happened when we presented our tickets to the usher as we were about to enter the theater. "Can I see your driver's license, please?" said the ambitious movie usher. The young man was exhibiting what I had always called movie usher syndrome.

Movie ushers are usually young kids, many of whom are given responsibility for the first time in their lives. They've been subservient their whole lives, to their parents, their teachers, and to other adults, and for the first time, they have a chance to order adults around. And they use every opportunity to utilize their newfound authority.

When asked for my driver's license, I had to think quickly.

"I don't have it. I left it in the car."

"Either you show me your driver's license, or you need to go back in line and exchange your ticket."

"This is ridiculous!" I exclaimed. "I'd like to speak to your supervisor."

"Not a problem," replied the cocky youngster. "I'll go get him."

A few minutes later the young usher returned with his supervisor, another teenager about the same age as the usher. "I understand that there's a problem here, sir."

"There sure is," I replied. "This usher is implying that I lied about my age."

"Calm down, sir. We can easily resolve this problem. Can I see your driver's license?"

"Why? You don't trust me?"

The supervisor's reply shocked me. "As Ronald Reagan once said, 'Trust but verify,'" replied the young supervisor, obviously wise beyond his years.

This was a phrase indeed made famous by Reagan while negotiating the IMF treaty with Mikhail Gorbachev.

The supervisor's reply caught me off guard, and I didn't know how to respond. I slumped my shoulders and just gave up.

I went back on the ticket buyer's line and eventually came

face-to-face with the young woman who had sold me the original ticket.

"Can I help you sir?" she asked.

"Yes. Thank you. I'd like to exchange the original ticket I bought a few minutes ago."

"Okay. Great. Would you like to see a different movie?"

"No, same movie," I replied sheepishly.

"Okay. Same movie but a different time?"

"No, again," I replied. My face was beginning to turn red.

"So exactly what do you want to change?"

"I'd like to exchange this ticket for another ticket for the same movie, the same time, but at a more expensive price."

"Oh my," replied the young woman, slowly beginning to realize what was going on. Unfortunately, the people behind me were also listening to this conversation and were also slowly becoming aware of my shame.

I walked slowly away from the ticket window, and in my mind everybody in line was looking at me. As Diana and I got ready to present my new, more expensive ticket to the same young usher, I felt like Hester Prynne from *The Scarlet Letter*, but instead of wearing a scarlet A on my chest for adultery, I felt like I was wearing a scarlet L for lying.

Having this humiliating experience in my rearview mirror, I was now ready to give the movies another try on the Thursday afternoon after I retired. I was also keenly aware that afternoon prices were cheaper and that in the afternoon, all tickets were the same price for all age groups. I wouldn't have to decide whether or not to try to buy a senior ticket and could thus avoid the previous fiasco.

We ate lunch and left for the neighborhood movie theater around 1:00 for the movie that was scheduled to begin at 1:30. We arrived at the Rio movies at about 1:15. When we entered the movie theater, I noticed several things.

First of all, there was hardly anyone in the movies. I was used to jam-packed crowds when we went to movies on either Friday or Saturday night, and seeing 90 percent of the seats empty was very unsettling.

Second of all, I was startled by the average age of the moviegoers on Thursday afternoon. Rather than a mix of young and old, like on weekend nights, the crowd was a mix of old and older! The average age seemed to be about 90. Diana and I were both 63.

Third, and most unsettling of all, half of the movie attendees that cold January afternoon were perambulating with the use of either a wheelchair or a walker. I felt like I was in a nursing home.

I removed my cell phone from my pocket and immediately called Matt. The coming attractions were set to begin in about five minutes. "Please finalize my contract," I pleaded with Matt. "I'll do anything to get to work immediately. I'll take half the salary that we had agreed on if that will help."

By then my voice was raised very loud, but I figured I wasn't disturbing anyone in the audience. I figured they wouldn't put their hearing aids in until the coming attractions started.

Chapter 25

THE GOOD LIFE

My contract eventually came through, and I officially began my life as a retired person working as a contractor to the federal government. The contract was for only half the hours I usually worked, so I had lots of free time.

Retirement was quite good. I had a contract with the EAC to do work that I enjoyed, and except for scheduled telephone conferences and travel, I got to do the work on my own schedule. That left me plenty of time to go to the gym and work out, play tennis and basketball, and read to my heart's content. I just had to spend approximately twenty hours a week working on projects that I enjoyed.

The new work was similar, but still different, from the work I had done at NIST. I was working with a different group of people at the EAC, learning how the various voting testing labs operated, and making sure that these labs were testing voting machines correctly.

I was apprehensive that working from my house would be difficult, since I really enjoyed the day-to-day interaction with colleagues. In fact while I was still a division chief at NIST, I was not a big fan of teleworking and allowed only a select few of my employees to telework from home. I felt that employees couldn't be as productive at home without the day-to-day interactions and feedback from colleagues.

Boy, was I wrong.

Even though I did miss the camaraderie, I found that I could get much more work done than when I was a supervisor at NIST. No one was coming into my office to ask inane questions, I didn't have to perform employee evaluations, and best of all, I didn't have to attend endless management meetings. Working from home was very productive.

Life was good.

However, I was getting older. The cold winters were getting more difficult to endure, and I started considering buying a house in a warmer climate.

I knew, however, that I would have to convince Diana to move.

"Why don't we buy a house somewhere down South?" I asked my wife.

"What? Are you crazy?" she replied. "We both hate Florida."

My parents had moved to Florida many years earlier and my mom was still living there at this time.

My dad had died on 9/11, but he did not die from the terrorist attacks. He had Parkinson's disease and lung cancer, and right before 9/11, he had been put on life support.

On September 7, 2001, my brother and I had flown down to Florida to be with my father, even though he wasn't conscious and couldn't recognize us. My mother really needed our support during that difficult time, especially as we were preparing to remove my dad's life support.

On September 10, 2001, my mom, my brother, and I made the difficult decision to remove my dad from life support.

We arrived at the hospital where my dad was on life support on September 11, 2001. There we would watch the staff remove the tubes that were keeping my dad alive, knowing that he would pass away peacefully a few hours after the removal of the tubes.

But when we got to the hospital, everything was in chaos. A group of visitors, joined by some hospital staff, were sitting in the lobby by a TV and were crying.

"I can't believe this," one of the visitors said.

"This is the saddest day of my life," another responded.

They were watching the terrorists' planes crash into the World Trade Center, a moment none of us will ever forget. But at that time I couldn't and wouldn't focus on that tragic event. We had gone to the hospital to allow my dad to die peacefully, and in my mind, I had to compartmentalize.

The nurses removed the life support, and we watched my dad take his last breath. Just like we were promised, it was peaceful. My dad was at rest.

After that event, Diana and I always associated Florida with the tragic events of 9/11. This association only added to our disdain for the Florida way of life. There were so many things about Florida that we didn't like. We didn't like the way old people argued over whether the cashier gave them the right change in the supermarket. We didn't appreciate the way the old people at my parents' condo would scream at my kids for splashing in their pool when we visited my parents, and we absolutely hated the early-bird specials.

"We need to go to dinner now; it's almost four o'clock," my mom would always say whenever our family visited them in Florida.

"But Mom, it's way too early," I would counter. "Can't we wait an hour or two?"

"What? Are you crazy? We'll miss the early-bird specials. You have to order before five o'clock."

For those of you that have never been to Florida and have not experienced this phenomenon, let me describe it. You get to the restaurant in the middle of the day to eat dinner, you order from a limited menu, and you eat the worst food you'll ever eat in your entire life.

But it's cheap.

Diana and I hated everything about Florida, and we always swore we would never live there, so when she said that we both hated Florida, she was absolutely right.

But I wasn't thinking about moving to Florida.

My best friend, Stan Willner, had recently moved to a small town right outside of Wilmington, North Carolina. It was not as warm there as Florida, but Diana and I didn't really want it to be too warm. We had always found the heat and humidity in Florida to be stifling. The summers in Florida were unbearable, but even the spring and fall weather was way too hot for us.

I had known Stan most of my life. Both Stan and I grew up in the "mean streets" of Brooklyn, New York. In fact Stan grew up in the same housing projects that I did—the Linden Projects. However, Stan did not live in my building in the projects, where Freddie lived, or the one next to me, where my friends Billy and Ira lived. Stan lived a few blocks away in a different building.

Consequently, Stan had a whole different circle of friends than I did. I like to tell people that Stan and I were members of rival gangs, if you can call a bunch of Jewish nerds playing stickball and "hit the penny" gangs.

Our "gang" would hang out in the park across the street from our building and Stan's "gang" would usually be in the schoolyard adjacent to the park. We would sometimes watch Stan's crew play stickball, and they sometimes watched us. But in the strange world of the city projects, we would rarely if ever speak to each other.

But we heard things about each other.

What I heard about Stan was that he always wanted to be a statistician for the New York (baseball) Giants. Even though most of us in the projects were Mets fans, some were Yankee fans and just a few were Giant fans. Even though the Dodgers and Giants had left New York by the time the Linden Projects were formed, some people clung to their team allegiance of first choice. Stan was loyal and remained a Giants fan.

Stan never fulfilled the dream of being a statistician for the Giants. Like me, he became a lifelong civil servant. We both started our careers working at DTMB, and Stan stayed at that job until he retired in 2002.

Stan was obsessed with stats. When working together at DTMB, Stan and I played on the same intramural basketball team. Stan kept the points per game average of everybody on the team, down to four decimal places!

"Stan, didn't you average 10 points per game playing for the DTMB team?" I once asked.

"Absolutely not!" Stan would answer. "It was 10.6679."

Stan never lost his desire to become a sports statistician and eventually fulfilled that dream (sort of) when he became the commissioner of our fantasy baseball league. He wasn't keeping stats for the Giants of major league baseball, but accumulating the weekly stats for our fantasy league would have to do.

After Stan and his wife, Maxine, moved to North Carolina, they would continuously invite us to spend a week with them. Maxine was not the warm and fuzzy type, but she had taken a liking to me.

"Mark," Stan would say. "As you know, Maxine is not very friendly. She hates just about everybody, but she really likes you." Stan would then spread his arms out wide and say, "I don't get it. I just don't get it!"

I didn't get it either. But I was very appreciative of Max's friendship, which supplemented the incredibly strong bond that Stan and I had.

"You know, Stan keeps inviting us to visit them in North Carolina," I said to Diana. "Why don't we take them up on it? We can use that visit to see if we like North Carolina and perhaps use that experience to make a decision about where to move," I continued.

"I thought you told me that your retirement psychologist told everybody that they should never make a decision about where to move after retirement based on where they go for vacation," Diana countered.

I thought quickly. "Ah, what does that psychologist know?" I countered. "He told me never to retire!"

Chapter 26

CAROLINA BLUE

We visited Stan and Maxine that year and every single year after that for seven straight years.

Each year we would look around at various subdivisions to see if there were any places where we'd like to live.

"There aren't any Jews here," Diana would say. "How can we move here?"

"When's the last time we belonged to a synagogue?" I asked her.

"About thirty years ago."

"How often do we go to synagogue, even to celebrate the Jewish holidays?" I asked her.

"Never."

"So why do we care about having Jews nearby?"

"That's the stupidest question I ever heard," Diana said, raising her voice. "Because we're Jewish."

"So, if we're Jewish, everybody we hang out with has to be Jewish?"

"Well, not everybody."

"How many?"

"I don't know. Quite a lot. Who am I going to play mah-jongg with?"

"All right," I finally relented. "Let's check to see if there are any Jews here."

We weren't sure how to do check for Jews, but one thing we did know for sure was that a Jew can tell if another person is Jewish usually just by looking at them, and certainly by talking to them. It's similar to a person's "gaydar," the intuitive ability of a gay person to discern whether or not another person is gay.

"Let's hang out with some of the other people who have moved here, and then we can figure out how many Jews are here," I said. I was very proud of myself for figuring a way out of this impasse.

Stan introduced us to many of his neighbors. We also went for evening strolls around Stan and Maxine's neighborhood and stopped everybody who was walking by and talked to them.

"What do you think?" I asked Diana.

"I haven't found one Jew," Diana replied.

"I have to agree with you," I responded. "But we've only spoken to a small sample of people."

"But we don't know anyone else to speak to," reasoned Diana.

A bright thought came into my mind. "I have a better idea."

"What is it, genius?"

"Let's drive around the neighborhood and look at all the lots that have just been bought. There are many lots that have been bought but the families haven't started building on them yet."

"What good would that do?" asked Diana.

"Well, the lots usually have a sign saying the name of the person who bought them."

"So?"

"So, we can look at the names and tell if it's a Jewish name or not. Don't you think that's genius?" Jews not only think that they can tell whether a person is Jewish by looking at them and talking to them, but they also think they can tell if a name is Jewish just by reading the name.

Oy vey.

We spent the next two days and nights driving around Stan

and Maxine's subdivision reading the names of people who had bought the lots. There wasn't a Cohen, Schwartz, or Feinstein among them.

"Back to the drawing board." I said.

The following year we visited Stan and Maxine again, making it the eighth straight year we had spent a week in North Carolina.

"I've got a new area to show you," said Stan. Stan anxiously wanted us to move to North Carolina so that he and I could hang out. "It's called Brunswick Forest."

Diana and I drove to Brunswick Forest along with Stan and Maxine. Brunswick Forest was a planned community that was scheduled to have 10,000 houses in the community eventually, and it was gorgeous. There were trees everywhere, with beautiful walking paths through the woods. In addition, Brunswick Forest had plenty of amenities, with tennis courts, basketball courts, and courts for a new sport I had never heard of called pickleball.

I fell in love with the place.

"What do you think?" I said excitedly to Diana.

"It's all right. But do they have any Jews?"

The clubhouse had maps on the wall of all the lots that were sold and the names of everyone who had bought them.

We looked at the names on the lots and we saw a Weinberg. Then we saw a Levy, then a Horowitz, then a Friedman.

"Look at all the Jews!" I said to Diana.

"There could be too many Jews," she responded.

My wife was never satisfied.

"Can't we buy a house here?"

"No," Diana responded. "All the kids and grandkids are in Maryland."

By that time we had five grandkids. Howard and Terry had blessed us with two grandkids—Kaela and Jansen, while Staci and Tony blessed us with three—Noah, Chloe, and Lucas. Almost all the Jews I knew had exactly two kids, so for Staci to have three kids was a violation of Jewish tradition. My father would never have approved. However, since Staci's husband, Tony, was not Jewish, the Jewish gods would forgive her, I rationalized.

The grandkids were the loves of our lives and each one of them was completely different from all the others. Kaela was very social and suffered from some of the same boyfriend crises that Staci had suffered through. Jansen was rambunctious and an "old soul." As an eight and nine-year-old he loved '50s and '60s music, and he and I would sing along to oldies in the car. Noah was quiet, and like most boys his age, loved to play video games. Lucas was a typical youngest child and was persistent, impatient, and creative.

Although these four grandkids played sports all the time, they didn't take the games too seriously. Whether they won or lost their games, they calmly moved on to the next endeavor. But not our fifth grandchild, Staci's middle child, Chloe. Chloe was probably the best athlete of the five and was by far the most competitive. She was a goalie in lacrosse and would bang her stick against the side of the goalie cage whenever anyone had the audacity to score a goal against her. If her team lost the game, she would brood about it for days. Chloe and I clearly shared that competitive nature. She hated to lose, just as much as I hated to lose. Show me a good loser, and I'll show you a loser.

When Diana reminded me that we couldn't move because all the kids and grandkids were in Maryland, I had already prepared an answer. "They can come out to visit. Stan and Maxine's kids visit all the time."

Although I was saying this, I didn't really believe it. I would miss the kids as well. We were so lucky to have them nearby in Maryland. We saw the kids and the grandkids all the time. "I have an idea," I said.

"Another great idea?" my wife responded sarcastically.

"Yup," I said, oblivious to the sarcasm.

"So, genius?"

"We'll buy a house here but keep our house in Maryland. We can come to North Carolina in the winter and some other months as well. We can even drive back and forth every month if need be. It's only a six-hour drive."

And that's what we did.

Our plan was to go to the Carolina house at the end of December and stay until the end of March. In the winter the average high in Wilmington, North Carolina, is fifteen degrees higher than the average high in the Maryland suburbs of Washington, D.C., where we lived. We also discussed which other months of the year that we would want to be in North Carolina, as opposed to Maryland.

We settled on our new North Carolina house at the end of June in 2014. We bought all new furniture and scheduled the furniture for delivery at the beginning of July. We scheduled the cable and internet to be installed the day after the furniture was to come.

But the day before our furniture was to arrive on July 5, it started raining. Then it rained some more, and then even more.

The rain that started on July 4 didn't stop until July 9. In fact, it wasn't just rain; it was a hurricane. Hurricane Arthur lasted from July 3, 2014, until July 9, 2014, and was the earliest known hurricane to make landfall in the state of North Carolina. What a way to be welcomed to North Carolina!

Arthur reached its peak wind of 100 miles per hour, making it a Category 2 hurricane.

Our cable and internet had to be delayed because of the storm. We were without power and without internet for the first five days in our new house.

I found out that when it rains in North Carolina, it literally pours there, not like the steady showers in Maryland. In fact it rained so hard then that in the six days during Hurricane Arthur, sixteen inches of rain fell, already more than doubling the July monthly average of 7.5 inches.

Stan had already informed me what the average highs and lows were in Maryland versus North Carolina in the winter and summer months. I had also researched those highs and lows myself, and I knew that the average temperature in North Carolina in January, February, and March was fifteen degrees higher than it was in Maryland. I also knew that the North Carolina highs and lows in July and August were exactly the same as the highs and lows in Maryland—72 and 90. But Stan had neglected to tell me what the rainfall was in both locations, and I hadn't thought to look that up.

A quick trip to the internet told me that the average rainfall in July, as well as in August, in Maryland was about 4.5 inches, but the average in Wilmington, North Carolina, was 7.5 inches.

I immediately got on the phone with Stan. "Stan, it's been raining ever since we moved in here. You told me all the highs and lows for the weather in North Carolina, but you never mentioned anything about the average rainfall."

"You never asked," was Stan's very logical response. Stan was always logical.

Chapter 27

STAN THE MAN

Stan Willner was the smartest person I knew. He had a photographic memory, and I can honestly say he was probably the smartest person that anyone knew.

Besides being smart, Stan was also almost always the nicest and most considerate person in the room—a rare combination indeed.

Stan knew just about everything. He loved and was a master at trivia. I had the privilege of being on his trivia team in a downtown bar/restaurant in Wilmington, North Carolina, called Hell's Kitchen.

Stan knew everything from pop culture to science to sports, particularly baseball. But perhaps his greatest area of expertise was presidents. He knew everything about presidents from the years they were in office to their vice presidents to the years they were born and died to their middle names to their wives' and children's names.

When the Hell's Kitchen trivia moderator would read the question, Stan would almost immediately wave his arms, tap his feet, and tell us the answer. On the extremely rare occasions when Stan was only 95 percent, rather than 100 percent sure of the answer, he was always gracious enough to allow one of the other dunces at the table, like me, to suggest an answer.

"I think I know this one," Stan would say. "But what does everyone else think?"

Some other guys on the team and I would suggest an answer.

Stan, knowing full well that we were almost definitely wrong and that he was almost definitely right, would graciously say something like, "Mark, that makes a lot of sense. Why don't we go with your answer?"

I would be at trivia only half the time, because Diana and I were only at our North Carolina house half the time. We were at our other house in Maryland the other half of the time. Whether or not Stan and I lived a mile away from each other, like we did when Diana and I were in North Carolina, or whether we were 400 miles away from each other, like we were when Diana and I were in Maryland, Stan and I still spoke to each other almost every day. We communicated via email, texts, and most often by phone.

When Diana and I were in Maryland, I would invariably receive a phone call or a text from Stan right after trivia ended.

"Mark, we came in second place tonight. We lost by just one question. We really could have used your help tonight. You would have made the difference. There were at least two sports questions that we got wrong that you would have known."

I knew that wasn't true and Stan knew that wasn't true. I knew a lot about sports, but if Stan didn't know the answer to a question, any question, it was unlikely that I would have known the answer.

But that was Stan, always wanting to make someone else feel good.

As I mentioned before, Stan and I knew each other since we were both 13 years old, both growing up in the mean streets of the Linden Projects in Brooklyn. We were extremely close friends for most of that time.

To be such close friends over such a long period of time, we had to have a lot in common.

And we did.

Stan and I discussed everything from politics to religion and spirituality to sports (including fantasy sports) to '50s and '60s rock and roll and almost every other subject imaginable.

I thought I knew just about everything about old music. I knew just about all the singers in the '50s and '60s and the names of all the songs they sung. I knew the year the songs were recorded and how high they climbed on the *Billboard* top 100 chart.

This was my area of expertise. I knew more about the "oldies" songs of the '50s and '60s than almost anyone alive.

But I didn't know more than Stan.

Stan and I would test each other every time we heard an oldie on the radio.

Here's one exchange that we had after listening to a song on the radio.

"Mark, what's the name of this song, and who sang it?" Stan asked.

"That's pretty easy," I replied. "It's 'Creeque Alley' by the Mamas and the Papas. The song tells the story of how the Mamas and the Papas were formed."

"Very good," said Stan. Then Stan asked, "How is 'Creeque' spelled in the song?"

"C-r-e-e-q-u-e," I replied, so proud of myself.

"Can you name everyone in the Mamas and Papas?" Stan asked.

"Mama Cass Elliot, of course; John Phillips; Denny Doherty; and Michelle Phillips."

"Excellent!" Stan said.

I always felt great when I received a sincere compliment from Stan.

"One last question," Stan said. "Do you know Mama Cass's real name?"

"Cass Elliot?" I said, my voice cracking, knowing that Stan wouldn't ask me that question if was that easy.

"It was Ellen Naomi Cohen," Stan said without a hint of gloating.

"Damn! I should have known that. My first girlfriend's name was actually Ellen Cohen."

Stan always knew just a little bit more than I did about old music. He also knew just a little bit more than I did about sports. But he knew a lot more than I did about presidents, history, geography, and almost everything else.

Stan and I were both very competitive. Although Stan and I were great friends, we competed against each other with great ferocity in many different endeavors.

Testing each other in old songs was one form of competition between us, and so was competing against each other in both fantasy baseball and fantasy football leagues.

But the competition between us started way before that.

Growing up in Brooklyn, we were on opposing basketball teams in the East New York YMHA (Young Men's Hebrew Association) league.

When we both stared working for DTMB, we were teammates on the same basketball team but still competed against each other to see who would lead the team in scoring. The older Stan was modest, gracious, and never bragged about himself. But the younger Stan was a lot different.

Although I ended up being the leading scorer on the team, Stan never let anyone forget when he scored a basket. After he scored, he would run up to the scorer's table, hold up two fingers and yell, "Two for Willner."

We were both a bit cocky when we were young and playing basketball on the same team. We would often get into shouting and shoving matches with some of the rougher basketball players on opposing teams. Occasionally the shoving matches escalated. If Stan or I would get really mad, one of us would act like we were going to throw a punch. But whenever we did, we were able to escape the punishment that was sure to come our way at the hands of our bigger and rougher opponents by yelling, "Don't hold me back" to the other person.

"Don't hold me back" was actually a signal to do just the opposite. If Stan yelled it, I would hold him back, and if I yelled it, Stan would hold me back. Thankfully this tactic always seemed to work and would deescalate the confrontation, luckily leaving us both in one piece.

On May 18, 2017, Diana and I were in our house in Maryland when we received a phone call early in the morning.

It was Maxine, Stan's wife.

"Stan's in the hospital. He's in a coma."

Diana and I were speechless. We couldn't think. We couldn't breathe.

Besides being the smartest and nicest man I knew, Stan was also the heathiest. He exercised every day, kept his weight down, and never got sick. Once most people reach their sixties, and certainly by the time they reach their seventies, they're on medication for multiple maladies, such as high cholesterol, high blood pressure, thyroid problems, or prostate issues, for men. I was on three different types of medications.

Stan was on no medication. He took no pills. He didn't need any.

The night before, May 17, Stan suddenly had trouble breathing. Maxine called an ambulance. Stan's heart stopped in the ambulance, but the paramedics got it started again; however, his brain had stopped functioning. He was brain dead.

The next day, May 18, 2017, the hospital personnel took Stan off life support, and he was pronounced dead.

I lost my best friend and the world would never be the same.

Chapter 28

THE GOOD LIFE—PART DEUX

To be friends for just about a lifetime, Stan and I had to have a lot in common. And we did. But in two things we were the exact opposites.

First, I had to pee all the time. It started when I was about 35 years old or so. My friends and I had formed a softball team in Maryland, and we played other teams in a county league. I arrived at the game a half hour or so before the scheduled start to warm up and, as I was fielding ground balls at shortstop, my position, I suddenly realized I had to pee.

There were no bathrooms at the softball field, so I held it in until about the fifth inning. The urge got so bad then that I had to do something. Luckily just beyond center field there were trees and bushes that would shield me, so I ran there between innings and relieved myself of that horrible feeling.

But that was just the beginning. Since that sunny day in 1980 I probably peed more than anyone else on the planet. At home, playing sports, and at work, I always had to pee. One time, while making a presentation to more than a thousand people, I had to tell the audience that we were taking an unscheduled intermission in order for me to leave the stage and frequent the bathroom.

My problem was so prolific that I was sure that I would not make it through the eulogy I gave at Stan's memorial without having to take a bathroom break, but I made it through. I think Stan, watching from up above, willed me through it.

Peeing every couple of hours was something that I just learned to live with. It was inconvenient but clearly not life threatening or injurious to my health, so I just accepted it.

Or so I thought.

It turned out that because my prostate had grown very tightly around my bladder, it had almost closed up the opening in the urethra where the urine flows through. Consequently, my bladder was filling up with urine and the urine was backing up into my kidneys. Just recently the doctors drained two and a half liters of fluid from my bladder and kidneys. I thought that I was peeing as well as I usually was, but it turns out that I was just peeing the overflow. That's why I could pee anytime I wanted to.

Luckily, draining the fluid out likely saved my life. After the fluid was drained, I had an operation to open up my channel in the urethra before it did irreparable harm to my kidneys. Although one of my kidneys functions at only about 20 percent capacity, the other one is 100 percent healthy. Since a person needs only one healthy kidney to survive, I continue to lead a healthy and full life.

Stan, as opposed to me, never had to pee. He just never did. If Stan and I were playing golf for five hours or on an all-day trip, I would never see him go to the bathroom.

"Mark, do you need to go to the bathroom?" he would always ask me, because he was so considerate.

"Thanks, Stan, be right back," was my usual reply. "Do you have to go?"

"No, I'm good."

To be honest I don't think I ever remember seeing him enter a bathroom. I'm sure he went to the bathroom, because everyone does, but I honestly can't remember seeing him do it. Another one of Stan's hidden talents.

The second big difference between Stan and me was our emotional makeup.

Stan was not very emotional at all, and I'm a blubbering idiot. I cry at movies, at TV shows, including comedies, and even at commercials.

One day when my granddaughter, Kaela, was around eight years old, I took her to see a movie on a Saturday afternoon. The name of the movie was *Bridge Over Terabithia*. I remember it like it was yesterday.

I know many parents and grandparents take their kids and grandkids to the movies regularly, and actually enjoy watching the movies that their kids and grandkids like. Maybe it brings them back to the simpler times and makes them think of the days when they were kids and had no responsibility. Maybe it just lets them escape the real world for a couple of hours. Or maybe they actually enjoy watching kids being kids.

I really don't know the reason why grownups often like kids' movies, but I do know that I never enjoyed watching kids' movies. And I have to admit, although I participated in many activities with my kids and grandkids, I didn't take them to the movies very often.

Thus, it was unusual for me to be at the movies with my eight-year-old granddaughter. I was thoroughly prepared to be bored out of my mind watching this movie, but I was enjoying the bonding experience that Kaela and I were having.

But this kids' movie was different. The plot was pretty good, and the movie was holding my attention.

The movie was a coming-of-age fantasy film with two young friends, a boy and girl, playing in the jungle. Then right in the middle of the movie, one of the kids tries to cross a rain-swollen creek in the jungle by swinging on a rope. The rope breaks and the young girl falls off and drowns in the creek.

Let me repeat this: In this children's movie, one of the main characters dies halfway through the movie.

So what did I do? I started crying. But because I wanted to seem manly in front of my stoic eight-year-old granddaughter, I tried hiding my tears and hoped that she wouldn't hear my sobs.

But she did.

"Grandpa, are you crying?" Kaela asked in the loudest voice I've ever heard her use. I guess she was so shocked to see a grown man cry that she asked the question again, in an even louder voice. "Grandpa, are you crying?"

Everyone in our row started looking at me. The row in front of us turned their heads around and also started looking at me.

I always knew I was emotional, but I found out then, and this would be reinforced later, that my granddaughter Kaela was very stoic. She rarely if ever showed any emotion.

I thought I'd never meet anyone as unemotional and stoic as my granddaughter, until I discovered that Stan's emotional make-up was remarkably similar to Kaela's.

I never saw Stan cry or even tear up, either at joyous events like weddings or at sad events, like when friends died.

I think much of this was because of Stan's ability always to use logic and reason, and by definition, reason is the opposite of emotion.

Stan rarely went to funerals, but not because he was uncaring. On the contrary, Stan was the most caring person I knew. It was because his philosophy was to get over the moment and just move on with one's life.

Being just the opposite, I was having problems getting over Stan's death.

"Mark, get over it," I could hear Stan telling me. "Move on. Live your life." That's what he would have wanted me to do.

At first, I couldn't continue to go to trivia at Hell's Kitchen in

North Carolina. I didn't really like trivia that much anyway, but I went there because I enjoyed playing trivia with Stan.

"C'mon, Mark, come to trivia with us," my friend Matt Klein told me.

"Do it for Stan."

It took me a while, but I finally realized Matt was right. I enjoyed hanging out with the guys.

I went back to trivia.

And I went back to life.

I started enjoying life again.

I had many friends, both in Maryland and in North Carolina.

Ironically Steve, of leather jacket fame, and his wife, Sue, who joined and then abruptly quit my fantasy baseball league, had followed us to the same subdivision in North Carolina, Brunswick Forest.

My boyhood friend Billy Epstein, who won the stickball championship in 1961, and his wife, Janet, live only six houses down the street from us.

Matt Klein, who convinced me to return to trivia, had lived across the street from us in Maryland but also moved to Brunswick Forest in North Carolina.

I had many friends in both North Carolina and Maryland and many things to occupy my time.

I was working, under contract, sometimes to the EAC and sometimes to NIST. I was enjoying my work immensely, and I could work from either house—the one in Maryland or the one in North Carolina. All I needed to do was to remember to bring my laptop back and forth with me when we traveled from house to house.

I really enjoyed my work, and I was being handsomely compensated for it.

I also really started to enjoy my leisure activities.

In North Carolina I was back at trivia every Monday night, playing on the team that we renamed "Stan Would Have Known That."

I loved to work out and went to the gym almost every day.

I also learned to play a new game that would eventually replace my work as my passion in retirement.

The game is called pickleball.

Pickleball is a sport played with a paddle, and it combines some of the elements of tennis, badminton, and ping-pong.

Two or four players use solid paddles made of wood or a composite material to hit a perforated polymer ball (like a wiffle ball with holes) back and forth over a net, with rules similar to tennis.

The game started during the summer of 1965 on Bainbridge Island, Washington, at the home of Joel Pritchard, who later served in Congress.

According to legend, Joel and his friends were bored one afternoon and attempted to set up a badminton court, but no one could find the shuttlecock, so they improvised by using a wiffle ball, lowered the badminton net, and made paddles from the wood of a nearby shed.

The derivation of the name, pickleball, is somewhat mysterious. Many believe it was named after the Pritchard's dog, Pickles, but others insist that the dog, Pickles, didn't come on the scene until two years later and that the dog was actually named for the game. According to Joan Pritchard, Joel's wife, the game was named after she said it reminded her of the pickle boat in rowing, where oarsmen were chosen from the leftovers of other boats.

I learned to play pickleball right after I moved part-time to our house in North Carolina. Brunswick Forest had eight pickleball courts, the most in the area, and pickleball was fast becoming the game of choice for older (and now younger) people in Brunswick Forest.

Pickleball was easy to learn and fun to play. I had played a lot of tennis, and I found the game to be similar but easier than tennis and more fun. The games were faster, and in pickleball doubles, which the vast majority of people played, it was common for all four players to wind up near the net with volleys that went on for quite a while.

My friend Billy Epstein and I entered an over-seventies tournament in North Carolina, and as partners, our team made it to the finals, where we traveled to Charlotte to play.

Pickleball was also becoming surprisingly popular in Maryland, as well, where I played in the county recreation centers.

Diana and I traveled back and forth between our houses, and the two of us enjoyed our time at both locations.

But we have more to do in North Carolina. I have pickleball and Diana plays in many mah-jongg games there.

Mah-jongg is a tile-based game developed in China and is a game of skill, strategy, and calculation, but also involves a degree of chance. Four women sit around a table, each with a card of various numbers and colors, arranged like a secret code.

Tiles are exchanged right, left, and across. The tiles are tossed into the middle of the table, and the players call out mysterious names.

"Three crack," says the first woman.

"Four bam," replies the second.

"Eight dot," says the third.

Finally someone calls out "Mah-jongg," and a new game begins.

Even though mah-jongg was developed in China during the Qing dynasty, for some reason it was played, at least until recently, mainly by Jewish women in the United States.

Mah-jongg has been played in the United States for at least one hundred years. From the city projects of New York to the bungalow colonies of the Catskill Mountains to the affluent suburbs of Long Island, mah-jongg, which had fallen out of favor in the 1920s, was kept alive by Jewish women.

Throughout the 1920s, the game was a popular craze but subsequently died out after some of the rules and regulations became complex and convoluted. After mah-jongg died out in the 1920s, it was revived in 1937 when a group of Jewish women formed the National Mah-Jongg League, which exists to this day.

The formation of this league still doesn't explain why the game was so popular among Jewish women.

There are many theories as to why the game was played predominantly by Jewish women.

One theory had to do with World War II. When their husbands were off to war, many Jewish women found mah-jongg to be an inexpensive way to get their minds off of the war, so they played it incessantly.

Another theory is that the Jews who fled Nazi Germany and made it to Shanghai got involved in the local culture and adopted the game. Once these women immigrated to America, they kept the game alive there.

Yet another theory is that the game was kept alive in part because it is a philanthropic moneymaking endeavor for Jewish organizations like synagogue sisterhoods and Hadassah chapters, who sell mah-jongg cards and receive donations. In order to sell enough cards, the Jewish women had to keep women interested in playing the game so they continued to teach mah-jongg to everyone they could.

My mother used to play mah-jongg constantly with her Jewish female friends. They played night and day. My mom played when she was in the Catskill mountains, when she lived in the Linden Projects in Brooklyn, and when she moved to Florida.

The women played right outside the bungalows in the summer

in the Catskill mountains or by the pool and inside in the winter. Especially in the summer, when the women were playing outside, their daughters would come by to ask their mothers questions. The moms would sometimes give the little girls money just to make them go away.

The little girls, to their consternation, ended up growing up to be the next generation of mah-jongg players.

A friend of mine who used to watch her mother play mah-jongg in the Catskills said to me, "We never wanted to be like those old farts playing mah-jongg, but somehow we ended up being our mothers."

I'm not sure how or where Diana learned to play mah-jongg, but somewhere along the way, she did. And, not surprisingly, at least at first, she played only with female Jewish friends.

I was working under contract, doing work that I loved and playing pickleball. These were my two passions that were getting me happily through retirement. Similarly, mah-jongg was Diana's passion that was easily getting her through her retirement. She played mah-jongg in Maryland, and when we moved to North Carolina, Diana started playing there.

There were only a few Jews living near us in North Carolina, but that didn't deter my wife. Diana found the few Jewish women living near us in North Carolina, and in what was then considered blasphemy, also began teaching the non-Jewish women how to play.

When Diana played mah-jongg in our house in North Carolina, I left the house. Although I have to admit that the women didn't seem like "old farts," I didn't want to hear the constant cries of "two dot" and "three bam" all night, so I would go out to a bar with friends or sometimes I would go out alone.

Once when I came back into the house, I saw of one the Jewish mah-jongg players sitting out one of the games.

"Doesn't it piss you off that the *goyim* are stealing mah-jongg from the Jews?" I jokingly asked.

The look I received in return was a combination of shock, concern, and amusement.

The next day I was playing pickleball with Suzie, one of Diana's mah-jongg players.

Suzie was on my team, and as we were walking off the court after we had won our game, Suzie looked at me and said, "Mark, I had a great time playing mah-jongg with your wife last night." But she pronounced it mah-JAHN, with the accent on the second syllable.

"Suzie, I can't believe you play mah-jongg with Diana and you're not Jewish. Furthermore, if you were Jewish, you would know that it's MAH-jahn, not mah-JAHN."

Suzie started laughing so long and so loudly that she could barely continue playing pickleball.

It took me a few years, but I finally figured out how to enjoy retirement. I always knew that for me, I had to keep busy.

Diana had to keep busy as well. I still work, on occasion, and I play pickleball and a little golf. Diana plays mah-jongg, a little bit more mah-jongg, and then some more mah-jongg. And just in the last few weeks I started teaching Diana how to play pickleball.

And she's enjoying pickleball.

However, as I write this final chapter, I haven't played pickleball in more than two months. I'm upstairs in my office in my Maryland house. Diana is downstairs playing mah-jongg. But I don't hear the tiles clicking or the loud voices that usually accompany her mah-jongg game. That's because Diana is playing mah-jongg on her computer, rather than in person, without real tiles and without real friends.

It's difficult to play pickleball and stay six feet away from your partner. It's almost impossible to play mah-jongg and stay six feet away from the other players and not touch anyone else or the tiles.

Yes, we're in the middle of the COVID-19 pandemic that has already killed more than 400,000 people in the United States and more than three million people worldwide. Economies in just about every country are in serious trouble and the unemployment rate is through the roof everywhere.

People are afraid to go outside and are trapped in their houses. When we do go outside, we're usually wearing cloth or surgical masks. The world is resembling one of those science-fiction pandemic movies that I would usually choose not to see. They weren't realistic, or so I thought.

By the time you read this book, either things will still be chaotic and deeply troubling or we will have this pandemic behind us. We all hope it's the latter.

I want to play pickleball again, and Diana wants to play mah-jongg.